MARKAYN
MARCHES

Drash

PROL IX

Heca

Kiybo

Arcas

GOLG REA

IOCANTHUS

Zillman's Domain

JOSIAN REACH

FENKSWORLD

of the ...cricord

Grangold

41 Pry

Woe

ANTIS BULA

Chyde Ten

Regulus

Cloister

PARASPINE

HAZEROTH ABYSS

Thron

IXANIAD SECTOR

Meridiana Saturus

Paul R. Beainos Jr.
9/14/11

DARK HERESY

DAMNED CITIES

ROLEPLAYING IN THE GRIM
DARKNESS OF THE 41ST MILLENNIUM

CREDITS

LEAD DEVELOPER
Ross Watson

WRITTEN BY
Alan Bligh and John French

EDITING
Patrick Rollins

DARK HERESY DESIGNED BY
Owen Barnes, Kate Flack, and Mike Mason

GRAPHIC DESIGN & LAYOUT
Kevin Childress and Mark Raynor

COVER ART
Clint Langley

INTERIOR ART
John Blanche, Adam Burn, Victor Corbella,
Simon Eckert, Imaginary Friends Studio, Aaron Panagos,
Aaron Kokarev, Igor Kieryluk, Erich Schreiner, Mark Smith,
Theo Stylianides, Tiernan Trevallion, and Kev Walker

ART DIRECTION
Zoë Robinson

PRODUCTION MANAGER
Gabe Laulunen

MANAGING RPG DEVELOPER
Michael Hurley

PUBLISHER
Christian T. Petersen

GAMES WORKSHOP

LICENSING MANAGER
Owen Rees

LICENSING & ACQUIRED RIGHTS MANAGER
Erik Mogensen

INTELLECTUAL PROPERTY MANAGER
Alan Merrett

HEAD OF LEGAL & LICENSING
Andy Jones

SPECIAL THANKS
"No Guts No Glory" Sean Connor with Mathieu Booth,
Nick Hodge, Karl Lloyd, and Stephen Pitson, "Bring the
Noise" James Savage with Dave Gallacher, Tommy Ryan,
and Stewart Strong, Benn Williams with Matt Fuller, Chris
Lancaster, Rebecca Williams, and Eric Young

FANTASY
FLIGHT
GAMES

Fantasy Flight Games
1975 West County Road B2
Roseville, MN 55113
USA

ISBN 978-1-58994-551-7   Product Code DH08   Print ID: 696OCT09

Printed in China

For more information about the Dark Heresy line, free downloads, answers to
rule queries, or just to pass on greetings, visit us online at
www.FantasyFlightGames.com

INTRODUCTION

"The death of a wanted heretic is only the beginning of our holy task, not the end. For the heretic can be found, can be killed—but in his wake, he may scatter ten thousand seeds in the fertile soil of human weakness that grow to strangle the future."

–Lord Inquisitor Caidin, Eulogies Vol. VI

DAMNED CITIES is part of the Haarlock Legacy Campaign for the **DARK HERESY** roleplaying game. This adventure features a number of different game styles, from survival horror, to intrigue, to investigation and desperate action. **DAMNED CITIES** can be played on its own without difficulty, but is intended to form the second installment of the modular Haarlock Legacy Campaign arc, and its use as part of this campaign should only serve to deepen and improve the experience both for players and the GM.

GAME MASTER'S BRIEFING

DAMNED CITIES is a murder-mystery adventure set against the darkness of the blighted world of Sinophia and in the decaying and corrupt city of Sinophia Magna amidst its viperous rivalries and festering hatreds. It brings the Acolytes face to face with murder, spite, greed, treachery, and warp-spawned horror, and ultimately reveals the lengths that the late Erasmus Haarlock was willing to go to achieve his terrible ends.

In format, the adventure itself is not precisely linear, but rather unfolding events depend on the course the Acolytes take against a backdrop of a steady escalation of the intrigues transpiring on Sinophia. Set against an increasing civil unrest and infighting caused by long-simmering tensions and brought almost to the boiling point by the very mysterious murders they are investigating, the Acolytes are free to pursue their own investigations based on the clues they uncover and the suspicions they form. Because of this fluid situation, the GM is required to respond to the players' decisions and shape the unfolding story and its outcomes accordingly. **DAMNED CITIES** in no small part has been designed with this in mind, and also features a detailed gazetteer of the city and world where the action is set, detailed background and character descriptions to help in this regard, as well as advice on running mysteries and open-ended investigations in your games.

DAMNED CITIES opens with the Acolytes assigned (or suddenly being reassigned—see page 33) to investigate a series of gruesome murders in the city of Sinophia Magna. These killings have malefic overtones, and their consequences for the world are far-ranging enough to provoke direct Inquisitorial involvement into what would normally be a local matter. Once their investigation gets under way, the Acolytes rapidly find themselves in an invidious position in which to attempt to carry out their mission. Although officially sanctioned, they are effectively friendless and unaligned to any particular faction. This situation is compounded by the rapidly escalating cold war between Sinophia's criminal underworld, its decadent nobility, and their corrupt agencies of control. Against this dark background of social unrest, urban decay, and growing turmoil, the Acolytes must steer a path between clashing factions to solve the mystery behind the killings, their cause and culprits—whilst the true power behind the murders gets ever closer to its goal.

Can the Acolytes save the damned cities? It's up to their actions and skills to decide.

THE STRUCTURE OF THE ADVENTURE

The ongoing events in Sinophia, the mysterious deaths, the tensions between the factions, and the daemon's ongoing quest to recover the mirror shards all have an impetus and attendant consequences of their own. Left to progress on their own, these events unleash the daemon in the mirror and herald the city of Sinophia Magna's collapse into bitter civil war and massacre.

The catalyst for change is the team of Acolytes, whose interventions and actions have the opportunity to solve the mystery, defeat the daemon, and avert the impending civil war.

The three broad parts of the adventure are formed as follows:

PART I: DEATH IN SINOPHIA MAGNA

The Acolytes arrive on Sinophia in response to reports of strange and brutal deaths. Upon arrival, they are plunged into the mystery of what and who is killing members of Sinophia Magna's nobility and underworld. As the mystery deepens, the Acolytes come face to face with the true nature of the horrific murderers stalking the city.

PART II: BLIND ENEMIES

As the Acolytes discover more of the malign forces and motive behind the murders, they find themselves in the middle of a rapidly escalating war between the city's criminal Undertow and cruel Sanctum Enforcers. The Acolytes must choose who to ally with and who to cast as enemies as the daemon's plans grow closer to fruition and the Acolytes are targeted for destruction.

PART III: THROUGH THE SHATTERED MIRROR

The treachery of Precinct Marshal Skarmen is revealed. The Acolytes may decide to stop the daemon's designs—no matter the cost—or to set it free by their own hands as the price of knowledge. Which will the Acolytes choose?

PLOT OVERVIEW

DAMNED CITIES is a murder-mystery, successful investigation into which uncovers a complicated malefic conspiracy by a trapped daemonic entity to free itself from bondage by re-assembling the broken mirror into which it was bound. Much of what follows—the adventure's plot and the schemes of the antagonists involved—exists to obscure these facts. That's the mystery part, after all. But for the GM who needs to know these things with clarity, the following is presented in bullet-point format about what is really going on, in order of occurrence.

USING THIS ADVENTURE

DAMNED CITIES is intended to take four to six play sessions to complete, and whilst there is some serious combat involved, investigation and involvement with the plot is far more important for success than simply how high a level the characters are. As such, DAMNED CITIES can be scaled to accommodate a group of between two and six Acolytes of any level of experience with some modification to the encounters, mainly by reducing the number of Risen the Acolytes must face if they are less experienced and by the inclusion of Spectre Cell 17 as additional antagonists for particularly strong Acolyte groups.

The adventure is largely location- and event-based, but the Acolytes' actions should have definite effects on the way that things evolve, and the GM is actively encouraged to add new encounters, intrigues, and NPCs, as well as modify or ignore the ones presented here as he sees fit. Bearing this in mind, the GM may also need to keep his players focused on discovering what is going on and nudge them back on course when they go too far astray.

Whilst the adventure can easily be scaled up or down by modifying the number of enemies to fit the group's capabilities, DAMNED CITIES is optimised for a group of Rank 4 Acolytes.

- Centuries ago, at the outset of his fratricidal campaign to murder his kinfolk, the infamous Rogue Trader Erasmus Haarlock summoned and bound a daemon in a pair of mirrors in Sinophia Magna (the capital city of the planet Sinophia) in order to question it.
- When he was done, Haarlock shattered one of the mirrors, imprisoning the daemon in torment to await his return.
- After Haarlock disappeared, the Folly (the tower in which the mirrors were held) fell into disuse and was looted, and the pieces of the shattered mirror were dispersed into other hands throughout Sinophia Magna in ignorance of their true nature. The artifacts entered into legend as arcane trinkets said to be able to foretell the future.
- Within the last year, the tower of the Folly was taken over by the beleaguered Adeptus Arbites detachment on Sinophia as their headquarters.
- At an ill-omened hour (see sidebar on page 21), all across the Calixis sector, domains and forgotten sins of the Haarlock line stirred in their slumbers. The daemon, its trapped soul and consciousness inhabiting the second un-broken mirror within a hidden chamber of the tower, awoke.
- Unable to leave the mirror or wield its full power, the daemon was, however, able to work on the vengeful dreams and deep-seated bitterness of Colchis Skarmen, the Arbites precinct marshal. The daemon slowly crushed his will into serving as the its malefic agent.

- From this point onward, the daemon and Skarmen have plotted to retrieve the broken shards of the shattered mirror, so that by re-assembling it, the daemon could free itself and escape before Haarlock returns from the void beyond.
- Using the warp-animated corpses of murder victims as their agents, Skarmen and the daemon have located and reclaimed many of the missing pieces of the shattered mirror, brutally slaughtering their former owners and any witnesses to conceal the theft and its true motives.
- As many of those who held mirror fragments were either members of Sinophia's decadent and jaded ruling class or powerful members of its criminal underworld, their unexpected and savage murders have upset the delicate balance of power between the two groups, leading the city to the precipice of civil war between the dissolute nobility and the powerful criminal underworld.
- As Skarmen schemes to recover the final pieces of the mirror and the city reaches boiling point, the Acolytes arrive. The Acolytes are called to investigate the savage murders and become an unexpected complication for all those involved.

Events after this point depend largely on how the Acolytes' actions and investigations proceed. On arriving in Sinophia Magna, the Acolytes are thrust quite literally into the middle of things, and although they have official sanction to conduct their inquiries, they receive little active help from the authorities and short shrift from everyone else. Depending on how they choose to proceed, the Acolytes encounter the various factions in contest for control of the city, each with their own vested interests and desires; whether these groups become allies or enemies entirely depends on what the Acolytes themselves do. At the root of it all is a concealed chain of evidence that points back to the shards of mirror and ultimately to Skarmen and the daemon. It is the Acolytes' task to discover this and thwart Skarmen before it is too late.

ACTION AND REACTION

Because Skarmen (the head of the Arbites) is in fact the culprit behind the killings, the villain of this adventure is in a unique position to gauge the success of his opposition. Should the Acolytes prove rapidly successful in discovering what is really going on, Skarmen can and should try to throw them off the scent with false leads, slow down or deny them official assistance, or set one or more of the city's factions against them. However, he is mindful of exposing his guilt, and he must be circumspect and always weigh the risk of discovery. His ultimate sanction is to act directly against them via the warp-tainted Risen, although he only does this when sorely pressed or when the unfolding events of the adventure reach a fever pitch (as represented in Part III).

MYSTERY, MURDER, AND THE GM

"The universe is so consumed by darkness that seeing the greater shadow of pattern and cause is a gift given only to the mad."

–Inquisitor Lord Caidin, in conversation with Cassilda Cognos

DAMNED CITIES is a mystery adventure in which the Acolytes work to discover the secret behind the murders that are occurring, eventually revealing the truth and confronting the hidden cause of events—hopefully averting a civil war in the process. This kind of adventure can be a challenge to a Game Master, particularly if he is relatively new to the twists and turns used in this kind of game, and so this brief section offers some advice about to handle mysteries in DARK HERESY in general and DAMNED CITIES in particular.

THE PATH OF THE ADVENTURE

As with many investigation- and interaction-based adventures, there is no exact "right" or "wrong" way for DAMNED CITIES to be played, and no single path to the successful resolution of the mystery at its heart. This said, some approaches are more effective than others in engaging with the plot, and indeed Acolytes who are too quick to "kick in the door" or anger too many of the city's factions at once are likely to—and indeed should—meet unpleasant consequences to their actions. Likewise, Acolytes who are too trusting—particularly of the local authorities and Skarmen in particular—might well rue the day they did so. However, Sinophia Magna should be presented as the dark and treacherous place that it is. "Trust no one" is an adage to live by for DARK HERESY Acolytes and should serve as a fair warning on a snake-pit of a world like Sinophia.

Open adventures such as DAMNED CITIES are designed to reward clever, imaginative, and involved players. Unravelling secret plots, pursuing the truth behind strange events, and uncovering dark conspiracies in this fashion are some of the core themes of DARK HERESY. However, care has been taken to add in action, some desperate violence, and horror as well. A mixture of combative and more cerebral characters should each have more than a fair chance to shine as the adventure progresses, and both brains, charisma, and brawn are likely to be needed for the Acolytes to come out on top.

GAME MASTERING DAMNED CITIES

This adventure has been created as a highly detailed framework for the GM to expand upon. As with any good published adventure, whilst you can of course simply run DAMNED CITIES "out of the box," the GM should always feel free to embellish the details and come up with new encounters based on what he finds here. Also, in any adventure without a fully developed structure, the GM should always have events and individuals react to the Acolytes' actions. This method always makes for a tighter story, a sense of empowerment for the players, and a better game all round. Because this requires a little more work than some more linear adventure styles and plots, it requires the GM to think on his feet, deal with the unexpected, keep a good idea of what's going on, and most likely take copious notes as he goes along! This kind of game, however, can provide some of the most rewarding gamemastering experiences. This is particularly true if the GM is something of a storyteller at heart, as he sees the adventure and setting he has created come alive in the imaginations of others.

VITAL LEADS AND USEFUL CLUES

In a mystery adventure, the players must discover certain pieces of vital information if they are to progress through the adventure to its dramatic climax. There is no point giving or holding back these pieces of information based on a bad dice roll. These crucial bits of knowledge are necessary for the players reach the conclusion of the adventure and either defeat great evil or be found wanting in the service of the God-Emperor.

Aside from these vital facts, any good mystery also contains a plethora of snippets, information, and minor clues that—while useful and important—are not show-stoppers to the game. These useful clues are like the pieces of a jigsaw; they give players a more complete picture of what is going on and perhaps certain advantages towards solving the mystery, defeating the villain, and a myriad other possibilities if discovered. Indeed, without unearthing a few useful clues, the chances of failure in any given adventure—particularly when antagonistic forces are acting against the Acolytes—may well be high, as the Acolytes may be ill-prepared or caught unawares at the adventure's climax.

In any mystery adventure, making a brief list of these two types of clues and leads can be extremely helpful for the GM ahead of time, as well as any that are made up as the game progresses. In DAMNED CITIES, this has already been done in the following section, but GMs should not be afraid to modify, add to, or subtract from these clues to suit their own game.

VITAL CLUES AND LEADS

The following are the key pieces of information the Acolytes can uncover during the adventure.

THE STRANGE NATURE OF THE KILLINGS

Sinophia Magna is experiencing a series of horrific killings whose violence is remarkable in its intensity and its perpetrators remain unknown. This lead pulls the characters into the mystery of the murders, who is doing it, and why.

This is part of their briefing, but more details can be given to them by Constantine when they arrive at Haarlock's Folly (see page 36), and by probing the deaths themselves.

THE NATURE OF THE VICTIMS

Both members of the Sinophian nobility and leading members of the Undertow have become victims of these murders. This lead pushes the players toward the conclusion that neither side is responsible and that they must have a common link.

This lead may be discovered at either the murder scene of Bal Grey or during the attack on the members of the Sinophian nobility (see the Corpse of Bal Grey on page 40, Death in The Clockwork Court on page 46, and The House of Amorite on page 50 for examples).

THE NATURE OF THE MURDERERS

Initial facts suggest that the assailants are phenomenally strong and are able to jam surveillance gear and move unseen through the city. Particularly adept characters may also deduce that they are somehow warp-tainted or even that they are animate corpses. These deductions may well lead the Acolytes into the diabolic involvement in the murders.

This lead can be discovered by making deductions at the various crime scenes and by talking to Lynan Yantra (see On the Run on page 46). A direct confrontation with the Risen themselves during the encounters Death in The Clockwork Court and The House of Amorite (see pages 46 and 50) makes the unnatural nature of their enemy clear.

THE TAKING OF THE MIRROR FRAGMENTS

The attackers were after pieces of mirror possessed by or linked to the victims. The involvement of the pieces of mirror leads the Acolytes to further discoveries about the mirror itself.

This lead may be discovered at the murder scene of Bal Grey, by persuading the Undertow to talk about the death of Callisto, from Yantra's testimony, or from the attack on the Judiciary (see The Corpse of Bal Grey on page 40, The Friends of Bal Grey on page 44, Death in the Clockwork Court on page 46, and On the Run on page 46).

The Fragments of The Mirror Are Tainted by A Daemonic Entity

The mirror's taint focuses the Acolytes' attention on the mirror and leads them to find out about its nature and origin. This lead may be discovered by talking to any who have come into contact with fragments, close examination of the legends surrounding them (in conjunction with Forbidden Lore Tests, perhaps) and most easily by directly examining the mirror fragments themselves—should the Acolytes obtain any.

The Fragments of The Mirror Were Taken From Haarlock's Folly

This lead ties the fragments of mirror, and the murderous attempt to recover them, back to Haarlock and to the Arbiters occupying Haarlock's Folly. The connection between the mirror fragments and Haarlock's Folly is revealed by contact with the Undertow or Sinophian nobility.

There Are Thirteen Fragments of The Mirror

This lead tells players who know that there is something trapped in the mirror just how close the daemon is to being free. The legend of the Folly's looting, a story known to the Rag-Kings of the Undertow, some in the nobility, and Eupheme Tassel (see Unvarnished Truth on page 50) helps the Acolytes figure out that there are thirteen mirror fragments in existence.

Useful Additional Clues They May Discover

- The uneasy truce between the Undertow and the Nobility is being threatened by increasing tensions thanks to the recent murders. Vox traffic is being jammed, random raids by the Enforcers are increasing, and cargo and assets belonging to the nobles are being attacked and stolen.
- The animated corpses of the attackers have autopsy scars as well as sorcerous marks cut into their dead flesh.
- A few weeks ago, Haarlock's Folly was struck thirteen times by lightening during a great storm; strange lights and sounds were heard from the tower.
- If identified, an attacker may appear on the official record as a recent murder victim gunned down in the current troubles and taken to the Arbites mortuary.
- Neither the Sanctum Enforcers nor the Undertow are commanding the dead; it is a third, hidden force.
- The risen dead (should they be identified or their remains recovered) have all already been killed, their bodies passing previously through the Arbites Mortuary.
- Certain information on the murders has been lost or obscured by the Adeptus Arbites.

FOR THE GM: A FEW WORDS OF ADVICE ON RUNNING MYSTERIES

To keep the adventure fun and fulfilling for all involved, the GM may find the following pieces of advice useful:

The GM holds the cards as to the mystery. Always know the answers; even if the players never get them all, the GM should always have them on tap. Reward good roleplaying, good planning, and good investigation with clues and answers, even if they only lead to more questions in the short term.

The players have the choice of what leads to follow and what inferences to take from their discoveries. Sometimes this leads them into paths and choices the GM hadn't counted on; other times, they'll just get it wrong. Try and respond to this reasonably based on what would happen logically within the framework of the game—a good understanding of the plot, the game's setting, or the adventure are fantastically helpful in this.

Change where clues and information may be found by the characters if necessary, particularly if getting them is crucial to the game. If needs be, the GM should move the location or event involved or provide a new mouthpiece character for these clues to adapt to a rapidly changing game.

Skill Tests and the like are there to add drama and nuance to what goes on in the game and allow the GM to make judgments on what happens; they are not there to punish the players or roadblock the plot, particularly in the case of a mystery adventure. If a particular clue or piece of information is vital for the game to progress, never make the players roll for it as a single pass/fail option. By all means, make the Acolytes work for it (or at least create the illusion of struggle to get it), and reward good investigation and role-playing with extra info and advantageous knowledge gained, but never let the game hit a brick wall because of a single failed dice roll if at all possible.

Respond to what the players do. Change the response of non-player characters so that the actions of the players have an effect on the adventure.

For example: In DAMNED CITIES, Xiabius Khan the Enforcer General may be helpful to the players if they have helped him in turn or appear to be open to bribery, but may become obstinate if he suspects that they are interfering in his business or even hostile if he suspects them of moving against him or if they've already fought his agents.

GMs should be fair, maintain tension, be consistent, and make things interesting and exciting both themselves and their players. Oh, and make notes—there's nothing more embarrassing than forgetting your own NPC's names!

THE SINOPHIAN GAZETEER

PLANETARY DATA

Population: No reliable estimate (estimated to be fewer than 150 Million, from a recorded previous height of 2 billion).

Tithe Grade: Exactus Minoris (planet unable to maintain regular tithe and placed under special measures as of 017.M41)

Geography/Demography: Temperate but unstable climate, remaining habitation centred on northern continent (Sinophia Magna: capital/starport, Karib City: lesser hive and industrial zone; population levels failing, Hive Argopolis: abandoned/unsafe). Sinophia also possesses extensive fertile wetlands and plains formerly cultivated but fallen to wilderness, lawlessness and widespread disuse. Sinophia's southern continents are currently evidencing extensive volcanism and seismic activity, leading to a planetwide increase in precipitation over the last several centuries.

Governmental Type: Oligarchy (Quorum of Noble Families)

Planetary Governor: The Judiciary Evandus Idrani, Seventh of his Name

Adept Presence: Adeptus Administratum, Adeptus Ministorum, Adeptus Arbites—All Minor (presence much reduced from former levels)

Military: The Provost Defence Army (Organized as a PDF or Planetary Defence Force, low/medium, declining, not considered fit for purpose under most recent sector strategic review), private armed cadres of the noble houses (small/medium)

Trade/Economy/Addendum: Legitimate off-world trade with Sinophia is limited. There is a long-standing boycott of the world by the Calixis Chartist Captains, although dealings with minor cartels and independents are frequent, if erratic. Thanks in part to its dwindling population, Sinophia is largely self-sufficient in terms of food and industry, particularly in scavenging resources of its former sizable infrastructure, although the heavy tax burden imposed on the population by the local government has led to rampant criminality and corruption, further undermining civil and economic stability.

CHAPTER I: THE SINOPHIA GAZETTEER

An all but forgotten backwater on the fringes of the Calixis Sector, Sinophia is an ancient and mouldering world of deserted cities and faded grandeur, a shadow of its former glory as an important Imperial world. Robbed of its population and trapped in an economic downward spiral that has lasted centuries, the planet is rife with petty corruption, apathy, and slow decay. Its remaining inhabited areas are a wasteland of neglect and partial abandonment, ruled by a bickering, jaded aristocracy headed by the Judiciary, a planetary governor in little more than name. Its people labour under the heavy burden of the taxes imposed on them by their dissolute masters in order to pay the failing Imperial tithe. Shorn of hope and empty of purpose, Sinophia is a morally bankrupt and outcast world slowly dying alone.

PLANETARY HISTORY

Sinophia was once a world of pivotal destiny and economic power, but now is little more than forlorn and forgotten relic of the past. Situated on the furthest reaches of the Ixaniad Sector and founded in elder days as the personal fief of the Rogue Trader Teresa Sinos at the end of her journeys, the world would (a millennium later) serve as a primary staging post of the Angevin Crusade that carved the Calixis Sector into being. In that legendary time, Sinophia was transformed into a vital way-station and a bastion of civilisation on the Imperium's then-frontier, its coffers swollen in the fulfilment of the crusade's needs and the booty of conquest, whilst men who would one day be cast as saints walked its gilded forums and warships swarmed its night sky. But as the centuries passed and the Calixis Sector coalesced into its own sovereignty and self-sufficiency, Sinophia's prominence began to wane as its purpose faded.

Increasingly sidelined and marginalised, much of its population—sickened by the excesses of the nobility—began to leave. Lured by the perceived freedoms of life on new worlds, they took up lawful passage as colonists. It was an exodus the rulers of Sinophia were powerless to stop, and as their world's decline accelerated, they fought back with the only means they had: money. They sought to set up merchant cartels, buy influence on other worlds through bribery, and out-bid competitors in lucrative markets. However, their struggle was ultimately futile. By taking on the new-founded economic and political powerhouses of Scintilla and the Chartist Captains, the Sinophian nobles had engaged in a costly struggle they could not hope to win, and in losing their trade war, they lost all. Major shipping routes were re-routed to bypass Sinophia, the sector governorship grew blind and deaf as far as the world was concerned, and its once-vaunted nobility found themselves burdened by crushing debts and bankruptcy. Sinophia was bought and sold; its cities slowly emptied and such recoverable assets it did have were carried off-world by rapacious creditors. Sinophia today is a world suffering the final throes of a long-drawn-out death by economic starvation and slow civil collapse. Criminality and corruption are utterly ingrained, and what little off-world contact it has is with smugglers, independent cartels (themselves skirting the fringes of the law), and a few hardy pilgrims. Whole cities lay deserted, and where Imperial civilisation does exist, it does so in twilight, clinging desperately to the faded glories of the past amidst the crumbling decay of the present.

THE POWERS THAT BE

Sinophia is a troubled world, but despite a long decline, it retains a sizable infrastructure and technological base that reflects its former importance. The nobles that retain power over its dwindling population do so with an iron fist, greedily wrenching every ounce of labour and coin they can from their downtrodden people. What remains of the planet's professional and governing classes are in a sorry state in general; its noble families, despite pretensions to grandeur, are functionally bankrupt, and maintain their station only by overstretched loans, underhand dealings, and off-world paymasters. Corruption is as endemic as it is rife, and theft, black-marketeering, extortion, and bribery are ways of life on Sinophia. Everyone from the lowliest beggar to the most coddled lord is on the take.

THE QUORUM AND THE NOBILITY

The two score of enduring noble families that remain of a once-great aristocracy are a fractious, petty, and cruel lot. Pathetic echoes of their illustrious forebears, they spend their lives in studied (and often faked) finery and indolence, indulging in decadent pleasures and spiteful courtly intrigues. Jaded and capricious, they scorn the 'ungrateful upstarts' of the Calixis Sector's distant elites—whilst each is secretly in hock to one of them or some other off-world interest. Some noble houses seek to prop up their withered fortunes by making secret deals with smugglers and criminals, and as a result, are locked in dependent relationships with the Undertow despite holding its members in hateful contempt. Others choose to live the lie that nothing has changed within the mildewed opulence and crumbling walls of their ancestral manses. The worst of their number have succumbed to malaise, spite, and madness; trapped in their decayed halls, they slip into spirals of malice that lead ultimately to ruin.

THE OFFICE OF THE JUDICIARY

Although the office of the Judiciary is also the planetary governor, in truth, this leader is usually as compromised as any other noble of the Quorum. The current Judiciary is no exception to this; Evandus Idrani is little more than a blustering figurehead. Pawn to numerous factions and bad debts, he has little control over his own court—let alone the thousands of Enforcers nominally under his command. The Enforcers are divided, corrupt, and unsubtle agents of summary punishment and social control, and most are little more than state-sponsored extortionists at any rate. At their core are the Mandato, a feared secret police force of torturers and killers that exists purely to maintain the Judiciary's power.

THE STATE ENFORCERS

The Loyal Enforcers of the Edicts of the Judiciary's Court are the law keepers of Sinophia. Their power is granted by the Judiciary and the Quorum. Therefore, by extension, they are sanctioned by Sinophia's dissolute and corrupt nobility. The Enforcers are intended to support the local laws of Sinophia, maintain order, and deal with such common crimes as murder, smuggling, and extortion, whilst the Adeptus Arbites, in theory, deal with crimes directed against the Adepta and those such as petty heresy, slaving, and corruption that contravene high Imperial Law.

The reality, however, is that the Enforcers are a brutal and corrupt force whose primary aim is the maintenance of the power of their noble masters and financiers. Though the various departments housed in the Sanctum go through the motions of investigating and punishing criminal activity, they always do so with an eye to their own—and their masters'—advantage. The head of the Enforcers is the vicious Enforcer General Xiabius Khan, a former bounty hunter brought in by the Quorum who has made the Enforcers a tool for furthering his own criminal ambitions and for brutally repressing any dissent among the opposition to the aristocratic rulers of Sinophia.

The Mandato

The Mandato are a division of Sinophia's Enforcers that function as a secret police force under the direct control of Enforcer General Xiabius Khan. Few in number, the Mandato enjoy a position of unquestioned authority and the ability to indulge any viciousness they please so long as it does not conflict with the agendas of Enforcer General Khan or the ruling nobility. Khan was given a mandate to form this division by unanimous agreement of the Quorum, who leaped at his suggestion to form a division to root out disloyalty and those who might threaten the stable government of Sinophia. As with all under his control, however, Khan has bent the Mandato to suit his own purposes, and they function as his own authorised cadre of vicious and ruthless monsters.

THE IMPERIAL AUTHORITIES

Over its long decline, the Imperial authorities have had little to do with Sinophia, partly because of manoeuvrings by the Calixis Sector's government to isolate the world and remove any outside avenues of support. Both the Adeptus and the Ministorum maintain a much-scaled-back presence than in more prosperous days. When Sinophia recently fell into arrears with its Imperial tithes—and despite its rulers pleading the effects of a failing population, poverty, and growing lawlessness in mitigation—the Imperium turned its face from Sinophia. Today, the Imperium maintains little more than token presences of most government operations on this blighted world. Assignment to Sinophia is not considered a mark of distinction for any branch of the Adepta. Indeed, more than one division of the Imperial apparatus has used the planet as a dumping ground for the incompetent, the ill-favoured, the suspect, and the lacklustre in their ranks.

The Adeptus Arbites

The number of Arbitrators on Sinophia has been dramatically scaled back in the last decade. Only small forces of Arbiters are maintained in the capital city of Sinophia Magna and the desolate, failing hive of Karib City. These forces are, however, extremely limited in number, having suffered serious losses in conflicts with the Logician cult during the Empty Men incident that have yet to be fully replaced. In Sinophia Magna, the destruction of the Arbites Precinct during the terrible events of the cult insurgency meant that replacement Arbiters have taken Haarlock's Folly on the outskirts of the city as temporary headquarters—though how temporary this arrangement truly is remains questionable. The only other manned facility in Karib City is chronically short of troops; those few remaining enforcers of Imperial law are housed in an echoing precinct fortress built to hold twenty times their number.

The Departmento Munitorium

Sinophia's diminishing population means that it can tithe a very few troops to the Imperial Guard, and the Departmento Munitorium maintains only a single office on the outskirts of Sinophia Magna. No Sinophian regiments have been raised for the Imperial Guard in more than four hundred years.

The Ministorum

Sinophia is an old world, older indeed as a colony that the Calixis Sector itself, and the Imperial Creed holds a strong sway over its population, but its cathedrals and chapels echo with congregations that are but a fraction of the great throngs that once filled their vast interiors. The priests of Sinophia tend towards weakness and lack much of the fire of the faith they profess.

The Inquisition

Sinophia has a long and infamous history in the record of the Calixian Conclave. Recidivists, cultists, daemon summoners, and hereteks have all ensured that agents of Sinophia have a deservedly tainted reputation in the Holy Ordos. However, the steady decline, general malaise, and outcast status of the place means that for some centuries now, it has had no permanent Inquisition presence in residence. Rather, it has been the subject of infrequent sweeps and programs of purging as the whims of individual inquisitors dictate and flare-ups of heresy have demanded. The most recent such occurrence was the bloody slaughter occasioned by the Empty Men incident.

As such, agents of the Inquisition are treated with general fear by the population, but most Sinophians also know that it is best to lie and keep one's secrets concealed when the Inquisition appears; no one on Sinophia is without something they fear being known. This can make operations by Acolyte cadres on Sinophia difficult, a state that is exacerbated by the dwindling presence of other arms of Imperial authority.

THE UNDERTOW

Organised crime on Sinophia is widespread, pervasive, and organised, with its main practitioners known in local parlance as the Undertow. The Undertow is as ubiquitous as the rain in Sinophia Magna, and has grown steadily down the years like a gorged maggot in the spreading rot of this benighted world. The Undertow's members are made up largely of the destitute and abused underclass into which many of Sinophia's workers, soldiers, and ordinary citizens have long slid. Together, they steal off-world shipments, trade in narcotics, and loot Sinophia's rotting carcass for gleaned morsels to sell to those who will pay. In the slums of Magna, they are the true masters.

Comprising a shifting quagmire of territories that make up Sinophia's remaining settlements and cities, the Undertow's shadowy domains are overseen by so called Rag-Kings and Queens, barons and lords whose titles mock the hated nobles of the Quorum. They control the black market (which thrives on avoidance of Sinophia's many taxes), gambling, narcotics, and prostitution, as well as offering murder for hire if the price is high enough. Many are also in league with off-world smugglers, corrupt enforcers, or are even secretly sponsored by decadent nobles. The worst are rumoured to have links to the dreaded scrapers and cannibalistic wrecker-gangs that haunt Sinophia's all but empty (and utterly lawless) outer reaches.

SINOPHIA MAGNA

lanetary capital and last bastion of the world's faded glory, the city of Sinophia Magna was laid during the world's settlement at the behest of High Captain Teresa Sinos to be her royal seat, and no expense was spared its creation. At the heart of a river confluence surrounded by fertile tidal wetlands, the rogue trader founded her city on deep-sunk black basalt foundations and crowned it with rose and white marble, sheerstone imported from far-distant Lys, and colonnades of statuary to echo the splendours of dimly remembered ages past. Inherent to its design was her own love of complex order and mechanism, and she laced it with intricate webs of canals and walkways, hidden plazas and winding labyrinths. Magna was built to appease her conqueror's vanity and provide homes for her favoured followers' families and their servants, whilst her imported population toiled elsewhere in her domain.

Unfortunately, history had something else in store for this jewel of splendour. Today, Magna is little more than a stained and faded monument to past glory, where sedition and vice take centre stage. Now the poor and the underclass crowd tenements cobbled together from crumbling mansions and dilapidated forums, whilst galleries of idle pleasures have been converted to ramshackle industrial units needed to maintain what's left of the planetary economy. Many of the noble families still exist, clinging mercilessly to their threadbare power and self-delusions behind guarded walls.

Since ancient times, Sinophia Magna has been divided into a number of districts; those of particular character are detailed briefly here. Further on, the GM will also find some closer descriptions of places and people of note.

DISTRICT I (PRIME)

The seat of power since the world's founding, the first district—or simply 'Prime'—is the centre of the web forming Sinophia Magna. The highest point of the city—the plateau hill on which the district sits—is in fact a beached star-vessel of Sinos' fleet graven from an asteroid mass and landed to provide a suitable foundation for the city's core. Its ancient reactors still provide power to the city a millennia later. Nowhere on Sinophia is its former power and wealth more obvious than in Prime, nor the decay and decline it has since suffered. Here can be found the Grand Basilica of the Judiciary House, the Fortress of the Provost Marshall (headquarters of Sinophia's much-diminished PDF), the Cathedral of Crusades Founding, the Administratum Ministry, the Gilded Exchange, and numerous monuments to forgotten luminaries and cenotaphs to the dead of the Angevin Crusade.

For all the district's monolithic architecture and intimidating grandeur, it is a forlorn and empty place where rot blooms behind ancient frescos. Buildings such as the vast Ministry once resounded to the scratching quills of ten

GETTING AROUND IN THE CITY

In terms of its transport infrastructure, Sinophia Magna is a tangled, half-defective mess. Whilst the wealthier districts and the commercia maintain a functioning, if haphazard, road network for the occasional rumbling cargo haulers, rickety personnel conveyers, and the liveried skimmer-carriages of the nobility, the rest of the city is filled with blind alleys, enclosed streets, and collapsed or unsafe roadways, making ground transport all but impossible. In districts such as the Sinks and the wharf areas, the canals and flooded roadways are the only reliable way to travel other than on foot, and these areas abound with motor-skiffs, mechanised silt walkers, and patchwork armoured barges.

thousand scribes. Today, however, they echo with the few hundred that remain, whilst the Gilded Exchange, once centre of interplanetary commerce, has been sealed and silent for centuries. The past holds many secrets in the Prime. Many mysterious factions and forgotten relics are hidden here, from the infamous oubliette dungeons beneath the Provost Fortress to the wondrous and inexplicable Clockwork Court at the heart of the Grand Basilica.

DISTRICT III (THE COMMERCIA)

Sinophia's remaining trading houses, reclaimator yards, merchant costers, and moneychangers are found in this rundown but relatively safe district. It is also home to the world's better suppliers and traders, as well as several small compounds belonging to off-world interests such as minor shipping cartels, salvage agents, and other independent operators, some of which are inevitably fronts for larger interests who could not deal openly here.

DISTRICT VI (THE GRANITE COLONNADES)

This district is better maintained and better policed than most in the city. It houses what passes for Magna's infrastructure and its professional classes—adepts and the like—and the businesses serving them, as well as a few Templum and alms houses, and the blackened and shattered wreckage of what was until recently the Adeptus Arbites Precinct fortress. The areas around the Sabbatine Bridge in this district also feature many of the more respectable diversions and entertainments available in the city. Many of Magna's largely untouched statuary colonnades and forums persist here, giving the district its more common name.

Sinophia Magna

& Environs

Drusus Flow

To Karib

Flavian Space Docks

Angevin Monument

Haarlocks Folly

Saint's Mouth

Whisper Reefs

Nemisis Sea

I, II, III, IV, V, VI, VII, VIII, IX, X, XI, XII, XIII

Key

A – Arbites Court House
B – Administratum Building
C – Seneschal House
D – Cathedral
E – Enforcer Sanctum
F – The Bridge of Tears
G – The Sabbatine Bridge
H – Karib Bridge
i – Sinophian PDF Barracks

DISTRICT VII (THE SHADOW MANSES)

With its seaward edge protected from the worst of the elements by a sheer cliff that darkens its streets in shade, the many fortified manses of District VII dominate the city's outer skyline. The heights are home to many of the remaining noble families of the Quorum, preserved in a decaying veneer of grandeur and attended by their dwindling private entourages, hangers-on, and hereditary servants. Despite the many bare and empty manses and overall impression of decay that hangs about the place, there is still wealth and power evident here, and death awaits the unwary would-be thief or looter. The nobility that reside here are every bit as paranoid about each other as they are the "filth" they consider beneath them, and encrypted ward accessors are required to pass even from one plaza to another in some places. The district is lit only by a handful of drifting glow-globes wending their way at night, and kill-rigged cyber-mastiffs roam the streets.

DISTRICT X (THE SAINT'S WASH)

By design, this area is most affected by the tidal influx from the Saint's Mouth inlet, and the buildings here are widely spaced, largely empty, and sparse in design. Many buildings have long since been converted to mausoleums and family shrines. Regarded as an ill-omened and unhealthy place, the district's only permanent residents are the Weepers Guild, a forlorn mendicant sect of the Imperial Creed who traditionally dispose of the city's dead by ritually giving them to the waters. These shunned clerics both live in and maintain the half-submerged tombs of the wealthy, and rumours have long abounded that their true faith is heretical in nature.

DISTRICTS V & XIII (THE SINKS)

These districts hold the worst slums the city has to offer. The Sinks—so named because of the amount of dilapidation, flooding, and subsidence that has occurred there—are a virtually lawless maze of crumbling tenements, flooded hab-blocks, labyrinthine canals, bridges, shanties, and open sewers

where few venture in from the outside. Here, the lords and ladies of the Undertow rule largely uncontested, and a man's life is worth less than a good meal in the commercia. Of the two areas, District V holds what remains of Sinophia Magna's working population, most eking out a toxic living gleaning scrap or taking on day labours for a pittance between long bouts of want. District XIII, however, is a different matter. Although little worse in appearance and easy to stray into unknowingly, it is truly a sinister and bloody locale, equal in danger to the worst underhives of major worlds, with many of its half-flooded and partially collapsed structures death to enter for the unwary. On Sinophia, a human has no further to fall than to be consigned to the Sinks of 'thirteen,' and it is said that anything can be bought and sold here—if you are powerful or dangerous enough to survive the sale.

FLAVIUS STARPORT

The city's starport remains active and in relatively good condition, although it handles far less traffic these days than it was designed for. The city's vox-grid and orbital control are maintained from here. Although still functioning, much of the starport's capacity and infrastructure have been shut down owing to disuse. Heavily decorated and ornamented in a high style, the multitude of landing platforms are covered in poorly repaired and moss-choked mosaics depicting the Rogue Trader Sinos' voyages, whilst its buildings are studded with looming winged seraphs and blazing suns rendered in weathered marble and tarnished bronze.

THE CLOCKWORK COURT

Beneath a dome of brass-latticed crystal at the centre of the Judiciary's palace is the Clockwork Court—a gracefully stepped open pavilion eighty paces in breadth. The Quorum, (Sinophia's elective council of nobles) meets here every ten years to select the world's ruler, as well as for one week-long session each month to debate, bicker, conduct spiteful politicking, and wrangle over courses of action seldom resolved. It is also here that the Judiciary, Sinophia's Planetary Governor (although truthfully little more than a figurehead) receives rare emissaries and petitioners.

To enter into the Clockwork Court, one must pass through one of the four grand entrance passages from the Judiciary's hall and loop through a maze of archive vaults, private chambers, meeting rooms, galleries, and cogitator stations. Many of these are now dusty and disused, and some areas are tellingly stripped of their former finery and equipment. One thing that Sinophia's decay has not changed, however, is the paranoid and thorough security demanded by its nobility. At each point, visitors are watched by armed guards and deathly still men with optical augmetics and high collared flak-robes.

Those who enter the court are waited on by clockwork creatures fashioned in the form of angels and heroes from Imperial history. There are thirty-seven 'servants' in the court. When not attending to visitors, they stand all but motionless, silently watching those who enter, following them with jewelled eyes. Legendary on Sinophia, these are

THE TRUE ORIGINS OF THE CLOCKWORK COURT

A thing of strange and sinister wonder, the most popular legend regarding the Clockwork Court's origins—that it is a legacy of Teresa Sinos, the world's founder—is, in fact, a lie. In truth, the Court was a thing fashioned and installed by Solomon Haarlock, the ancient rival of the Sinos and once a brutal oppressor of Sinophia in the forgotten past. It was Haarlock who first established the Court and determined that the nobles of Sinophia would be mere gears in his machine. Despite these facts being deeply buried and conveniently forgotten even by the nobles (although the likes of Eupheme Tassel know the truth, at least in outline—see page 25), Acolytes who have encountered the Haarlock line's fascination with such mechanisms and their sometimes deadly power before (either thanks to House of Dust and Ash or **Tattered Fates**) may very quickly suspect the truth themselves. The Court itself, however, has nothing to do with the murder mystery, making it a quite deliberate red herring as to what's really going on…

no mere servitors, for they contain no flesh. Each is a wonder of glittering brass, charged copper, and brushed steel, their movements pulsing with soft clicks and whirs. The floor of the court is transparent and reveals the vast whirling mechanism beneath that powers and controls the servants. The workings of the court's mechanism are a mystery, and it has run without fail since the world's foundation. Some whisper that the Clockwork Court controls some ancient secret—a legacy of the Rogue Trader Teresa Sinos.

THE SANCTUM

The Granted Sanctum of the Loyal Enforcers of the Edicts of the Judiciary's Court is a large, mouldering collection of connected town houses in District III. The buildings are in poor repair; plaster flakes away from walls and the wooden stairs and doors are heavy with damp. Bundles of cogitator cable punch through walls and crowd doors, and most offices are cramped with piles of mildewed dockets. These upper levels house various offices, chief of which are the Office of Political and Moral Affairs in a set of converted reception rooms, the Office of Fiscal Affairs (also known quietly as the "ministry of theft") in the draughty roof levels, and the dreaded Office of Civil Order occupying a former ballroom. Scattered throughout the building are various other minor offices: the central armoury, firing ranges where crumbling statuary are used as targets, public cages, vehicle yards, stores, and landing pads for the Enforcers' hover transports and gunships.

The upper levels are dismal and fearful. However, it is below ground that the true heart and terror of the Sanctum lays, behind plasteel doors in mouldering passageways bathed in the sickly yellow light of rigged glow globes. Here, Enforcer General Xiabius Khan keeps office as head of the feared Mandato. On these levels, the questioners ply their trade in rooms carefully painted in deep, gloss red, whilst hidden vaults house higher-grade cogitator units, med bays, a well-stocked armoury, and comm-relays. Khan's personal offices and living quarters are also located here, a suit of rooms decked out in a painfully crass high style that is the former bounty hunter's taste.

THE TURNING HAND

The Turning Hand on the edge of the Commercia is the oldest meeting house on Sinophia. Said to have existed for more than a millennia, it has succumbed by inches to the Sinophian malaise. During the centuries of prosperity, merchants, traders, information gleaners, and other fortune-seekers would meet in the Turning Hand's golden halls to exchange information, eat, drink, and mingle in the incense-fogged atmosphere. However, the death of trade and Sinophia's isolation and decline doomed the Hand. People still come to trade and deal in whispers, but the bustle of the place is long gone. The alcove tables are not filled, one does not make reservations for private dining, and most of the tarot tellers for which the Hand was famed are absent, their veiled enclaves unneeded when the fortunes of Sinophia are so clear. The Hand has now become the ill-lit haunt of what few off-worlders come to Sinophia. Here, one is likely to find agents of foreign cartels, far travellers, and silent strangers sipping spiced amasec and muttering discussions amid the empty spaces and echoing salons. Gossip and rumours run though the Turning Hand like a river; most are highly dubious but many are at least partially accurate.

The Hand's great central chamber, is a richly decorated (but long-faded) domed room dominated by seven great pillars, each ten times the height of a man and glittering with tarnished golden fume pipes pumping incense into the air. Meanwhile, faces of cards from the Emperor's Tarot—enamelled on brass sheets—rotate on chains dangling from the painted ceiling. Designed to hold hundreds, the chamber seems now oppressively silent and ill-lit, its high stained-glass windows shrouded in grime and rainwater. A circular bar fills the centre of the crimson carpeted floor. There, the owner (a plump, elderly man known as Master Brazen Thall) lords over decrepit-looking servitors. Thall's easy manner and good-natured absentmindedness conceals a wit and will undimmed by time, and he misses little.

THE CELESTINE WHARF

Upstream from the mouth of Drusus' Flow is a stagnant side spur sluggishly flowing through the city's notorious District XIII. The spur was long ago shaped and constrained into a dead-end canal for unloading river barges. This strip of foul-filmed water is shadowed by the close press of warehouses, from which loading spars spill their rusting chains to water

SETTING THE SCENE IN SINOPHIA MAGNA

Characters in Sinophia will be struck by a number of things: Sinophia is in a state of slow decay, and everything is a relic of an older, grander time on the verge of giving itself up to ruin. Brickwork sags; paving slabs are cracked and uneven; water spills out of cracks and runs down walls; rust and tarnish taint every piece of exposed metalwork. The city of Sinophia Magna is made of natural materials gone to rot, rust, or tarnish: plaster, wood, paint and (in the case of nobles) marble, stucco, and gilt, granting the city a universal smell of damp, decay, and mustiness. In poorer districts the stench of refuse, sewage, and stagnant water dominate, occasionally interspersed with the smells of bland, boiled food and scented narc-smoke. In more opulent surroundings, thick (often sickly) perfumes and incense are used to cloak the underlying reek.

It's a truism (particularly among visitors) that it always rains in Sinophia Magna, and whilst this is not strictly, true the rain should always be a feature of your games. The rain may change at a moment's notice from a omnipresent drizzle to a torrential downpour, bringing ankle-high rivers gushing through the streets. Loneliness and desertion is also a key factor to convey, particularly in contrast to other Imperial worlds the Acolytes may have travelled to. Hab-stacks stare vacant and empty with smashed-window eyes, sounds are infrequent and strange, echoing plaintively through canyons of deserted ferrocrete. Out on the veldt and stonelands, horizons stretch for miles without sight of human life, here and there dotted with the rusted and crumbling relics of the past.

THE SINOPHIAN MENTALITY

Malaise, melancholy, and corruption (in both the mundane and esoteric senses) are the abiding qualities of the Sinophian people—hope is simply a word, faith and ambition are the subjects of quiet, bitter mockery, and selfishness is viewed as a survival trait. Sinophians are, to put it bluntly, a morose, fearful, self-absorbed, vicious, and untrustworthy lot in general, and usually assume everyone else is the same. There are obviously plenty of exceptions to this stereotype, both good and bad, and perhaps the most dangerous of them are the ones who genuinely have found a cause to believe in, because they often take to it with the fanaticism of a true convert.

AN EXAMPLE SINOPHIAN SCENE

As an example of how these qualities can be used, here is an example of a description of meeting a Sinophian noble in his private library. As a scene-setter, the description here is somewhat heavy-handed, but GMs will appreciate the attention to detail:

The room is dark. Weak light enters through the dusty panes of an ill-repaired grand window, through which can just be seen the rain-wetted roofs of the city. Bowing wooden shelves line the walls from floor to smoke-yellowed ceiling. The shelves are a jumble of mildewed books with cracked leather covers. A scattering of aged portraits and busts, dusty and cobwebbed, can be seen in a few of the niches in the book shelves, whilst the room's few other furnishings are concealed under stained covers. The smell of must is thick in the air, and the floor is covered in threadbare carpets which send up small plumes of dust with each step you take.

You see the nobleman seated as still and pale as a corpse by a cold fireplace. His elaborate drape jacket might once have been a rich red velvet, but now has stained and faded to the colour of dry blood. Dark jewels and gold rings adorn his gloved hands, and his face is painted in the thick white courtly makeup of centuries past. He studies you with almost feverishly bright eyes and as he speaks the paint cracks and flakes around his mouth, giving the disturbing impression that his face is splitting open.

at high tide. It is said that when it was built, the merchants commissioned a statue of the blessed Saint Celestine by the finest craftsman and sunk it to the depths of the canal so that she could watch over the waters and bring them fortune.

The dock is long unused, and its bays are crammed with rusted cargo barges, whilst its warehouses are the haunts of dregs and gangs. Riddled with connections to the half-flooded sewage system beneath the city and canals, the Undertow may pass here unseen, and many warehouses surrounding the docks are utterly in their control. Various Rag-kings use them as places to store contraband or host illegal slave fights and beast games. The dock waters are a notorious place to be 'sent to meet the saint" by weighting one's feet and throwing them alive into the waters.

The statue itself is enormous, pitted and overgrown with algae. However, its shape is still faintly discernible. Its position (lying in the channel just off the docks and wharfs) means that most traffic over the dock passes over the statue. It is considered fortunate to gain "the blessings of the Saint" by taking this route.

HAARLOCK'S FOLLY

On the northwest outskirts of Sinophia Magna's District VII sits Haarlock's Folly. Built long ago by the Haarlock line this high tower sits on a jutting promontory of rock above the waters of Saint's Mouth and glowers down at the rotting city. Following the disappearance of Erasmus Haarlock over a century ago, the Folly has been looted. Until recently, it was home to little more than dust, cobwebs, and such clocks and fittings that could not easily be carried away.

In recent years, Haarlock's Folly was commandeered by Sinophia Magna's small force of Adeptus Arbites. This force of less than forty Arbitrators and auxiliaries were sent as a fresh replacement detachment following the destruction of the original Arbites precinct fortress during the Logician plot known to the Inquisition as the Empty Men of Sinophia Magna. This force, under Precinct Marshal Colchis Skarmen, has converted the Folly's empty chambers into a makeshift headquarters and its cellars to incarceration cells, autopsy morgues, and armouries.

II

WICKED CITY

CHAPTER II: WICKED CITY

The following section represents some in-depth background for the adventure and the factors and factions involved in it.

SINOPHIA MAGNA

The world of Sinophia is a troubled backwater world, only nominally part of the Calixis Sector. It is ancient, corrupt, and slowly dying of deliberate economic starvation for many centuries. Its capital and seat of power is Sinophia Magna, a once-glorious city that has long since succumbed to slow malaise and terminal decline. Sinophia Magna is a key character in its own right, and serves as a backdrop against which the GM is encouraged to add his own encounters, characters, and events. A detailed gazetteer for Sinophia focusing on Sinophia Magna and its society can be found on page 10.

THE BALANCE OF POWER

The balance of power on Sinophia is a delicate one, and for off-worlders (such as the Acolytes are likely to be), the situation here is likely to seem frighteningly unstable compared to a long-established Imperial world. To an outsider's point of view, the bloody-handed grip of Sinophia's decaying nobility seems shockingly precarious on close inspection, whilst the power of its criminal underclasses (most clearly in the shape the highly organised Undertow who govern the slums and part-flooded alleyways of Magna itself) seems rampant. Both sides of this precarious balance despise and distrust the other, but stop short of mutual destruction by common need. They avoid all-out conflict by using tangled webs of debt, vendetta, and fear. The recent spate of murders of powerful players on both sides of Sinophia's divide has threatened to end this status quo and plunge Magna into bloodshed and anarchy.

The power of the Imperium's own organisations on Sinophia are in a similarly perilous state. The Arbiters are too few in number and are all but sidelined by the political manoeuvrings around them, whilst the Adepta have long used this outcast world as a dumping ground for their least favoured and most lacklustre servants. Thus, the Imperium's own institutions on Sinophia have withered over the years to their present condition as vain, self-absorbed, and all but powerless shadows of what they might have been.

As a result of generations of incompetence, malignancy, and bitterness on the part of those who rule over their lives, the common Sinophians themselves have borne the brunt of their world's slide into slow death and have become a maudlin and often macabre breed, prone to despair, faithlessness, and (when pushed too far) revolt. They are, however, little deserving of the suffering they must endure daily.

THE DAEMON AND ITS WORKS

The trapped daemon in the mirror is focused entirely upon gaining its freedom, and does not care who dies in the process or how this is achieved. It also knows that it must act soon, for it feels that its master will soon return, an event that even its hellish heart dreads. Using Skarmen as its proxy, the daemon has determined to retrieve the mirror fragments and free itself, crushing his will and fanning the flames of hatred Skarmen bore toward both the nobility and the Undertow to the point where his own hatreds have unhinged and corrupted him.

Using rituals daemon-whispered in his ear, Skarmen has animated the corpses stolen from the Arbites precinct mortuary and sent them out to do murder and retrieve the shard fragments. These deaths have created a steadily rising tide of suspicion, anger, and reprisal in the city, with neither the nobility nor the Undertow knowing who is really to blame. Now that the daemon's goal is drawing close, outside forces threaten to intervene. Only a few more mirror shards remain to be seized, and the daemon pushes Skarmen even harder in its service, risking catastrophe and exposure in order to gain its freedom.

THE ADVENTURE BACKGROUND IN DETAIL

On the planet of Sinophia in the distant past, the infamous Rogue Trader Erasmus Haarlock bound in secret a daemonic warp-entity of great power between two mirrors facing each other. The paired mirrors were wrought of forbidden sorcery and ancient xenos technology wedded together by Haarlock's own twisted genius. Whilst held in this insubstantial gaol, Erasmus Haarlock put the helpless daemon to the question, first on where the last of his treacherous kin could be found, and later (once they had been hounded to extinction), he sought to pry from it other, darker secrets. The daemon was wracked by every sorcerous art and device that the power of Haarlock could command. At length, pleasing lies, vile truths, and many more revelations besides poured from its lips. Yet even in its answers

USING THE ADVENTURE BACKGROUND

This section contains a detailed account of the malign events, including the binding of the daemon in the mirror and the corruption of Marshal Skarmen, and this back-story sets the stage for what is to come. This history can be used by the GM as a basis to create his own additional clues, leads, and encounters. Although all of these things occur before the Acolytes' involvement in the matter—and indeed the entire adventure could be successfully completed without the Acolytes discovering the truth of why the dark conspiracy has occurred—knowing the cause of events is invaluable for any mystery in order to give it motive, coherence, and depth.

THE MOMENT HAARLOCK'S FOLLY CAME ALIVE

The mysterious events in Haarlock's Folly and the awakening of the daemon are just a few in a series of events across the Calixis Sector connected with the Haarlock bloodline. Artefacts, servants, and old domains stir as if performing some kind of pre-set operation or presaging approaching doom. These phenomena, the nightmarish events that seem to be catalysed by them, and the Inquisition's response all form the keystones of the Haarlock Legacy campaign.

If DAMNED CITIES is the first adventure the GM has run from the campaign, he can keep any connection with other events vague, as it will likely only confuse matters at this point, or ignore them entirely. If, however, the GM has run either TATTERED FATES or The House of Dust and Ash (see DISCIPLES OF THE DARK GODS page 198) first, he may want to have the storm at the Folly coincide with either time the Grand Conjunction (see TATTERED FATES, page 54 for more details), or with the moment that the Gilded Widow comes alive (see page 219 of DISCIPLES OF THE DARK GODS). This will make what is happening in Sinophia Magna part of a wider pattern and reinforce in the players' minds that the events here are merely part of a wider, darker pattern. Conversely of course, the GM may wish to place the storm at the Folly first in this chronology, as the heralding echo of Haarlock's return here first entering the warp-given visions of the Beloved from TATTERED FATES and speaking in dreams to the servants of the House of Dust and Ash.

Erasmus Haarlock found only more questions and other doors to open in his quest for the impossible. Thus, in contempt, he discarded the bound daemon to seek his answers elsewhere. Haarlock broke one of the pair of arcanely fashioned mirrors, shredding the daemon's form and fixing its malefic essence helpless in place in the remaining intact mirror. The daemon screamed silently in vain from its slivered prison, cursing and at the same time fearing the return of its tormentor.

Decades later, Haarlock disappeared beyond the edge of what was known and passed into legend. On Sinophia (where the Haarlock line had long been the subject of resentment and fear), the nobles conspired to use pawns to break open Haarlock's tower. Although the defensive measures within the structure (known afterwards as Haarlock's Folly) claimed the lives of many of their first agents, the tower was soon ransacked and looted in a free-for-all by the dissolute and avaricious nobles and the criminal masters of Sinophia's underworld. The shards of the broken mirror were taken by thieves and changed hands over the years afterwards as wondrous and forbidden things able to afford glimpses of the future and other such blasphemous tricks. The daemon's essence, however, remained bound to the intact mirror that hung draped in black cloth in a secret chamber in the Folly. Thus, both mirror and daemon were undiscovered by the robbers and brooded in malevolent silence for many years.

THE EMPTY MEN

The Empty Men of Sinophia Magna was a Logician-sponsored project that sought to corrupt humans with aspects of the alien at the genetic level. The Logicians had secretly taken over control of the PDF Medicae facility in Sinophia Magna and were using demobilised PDF troopers as unwitting test subjects for gene-altering viruses. Almost all the strains tested on the unwitting troopers were highly unstable and in most cases killed the test subject. In some cases, however, it led to violent mental breakdown and catastrophic genetic meltdown. There were a few successes—the Logicians created a handful of functioning transgenic blasphemies that were later dubbed the 'empty men' by the Inquisition. Most of these unfortunate test subjects were recovered by agents seeded within the Adeptus Arbites stationed on Sinophia, who also ensured that the project remained unnoticed by the authorities.

When the heretical project was discovered, the Logicians put into effect one of their trademark apocalyptic exit plans. The PDF barracks were saturated with psychoactive chemicals. This reduced the garrison to crazed killers that slaughtered each other and anyone who they came into contact with. The Logician agents secreted within the Arbites overloaded the plasma reactor beneath the Adeptus Arbites Precinct, reducing it to molten slag and killing ninety percent of the garrison. The surviving Arbites and a handful of agents of the Inquisition stormed the PDF Medicae facility. They discovered hidden laboratories beneath them and horrors that were held within. Though most of the Logician agents were either killed or captured, some believe that the Logicians succeeded in extracting the keys to their limited success and that on some unknown world, more empty men are being created as the Logician's plans creep towards fulfilment.

THE DAMNED CITIES CONNECTION

In Damned Cities, the Empty Men incident plays no direct part. It is part of the setting of Sinophia Magna that is intended to make it feel more exiting and real to the players. It is the reason why the Arbites are housed in Haarlock's Folly, undermanned and disconsolate. It also informs why the events of the adventure cause panic to the city; in that many may believe that it is the Empty Men incident literally happening all over again.

Over the years that followed, the tower of the Folly remained empty and disused, a far from uncommon occurrence on decaying Sinophia. It rapidly drew a reputation as being haunted or accursed, and not even the Undertow's members would countenance the idea of using it. Then (a little less than a year ago), as if sent by a malign providence, Haarlock's folly was commandeered by the Adeptus Arbites in the aftermath of the affair that became known as the Empty Men incident. During this episode, the heretical experiments of the recidivist tech-cult known as the Logicians resulted in a terrorist attack which destroyed the former Arbites Precinct House, and along with it many of the planet's small Arbites detachment. The remaining Arbiters found themselves manipulated into occupying the accursed Folly by the ruling Quorum as a temporary measure to replace their lost headquarters. The nobles slyly congratulated themselves at what they saw as a calculated insult to meddling Imperial authority, little guessing that the barb would later come to cost them all dearly.

On a dark and storm-lashed night, Haarlock's Folly seemed to come alive; baleful lights crackled across the tower's upper reaches and Arbiters rose to arms against what they thought was a sudden attack, as noises like the screaming of a tormented souls were heard on the wind. Throughout the city, thousands awoke choked by fearful nightmares they could not remember. That night, the Folly was struck thirteen times by lightning, and ancient gears and clockwork frozen for decades began to shift and move. Within the sealed chamber, the shrouding black drape fell partly away, and the daemon stared out from within.

As the storms across Magna raged for a dozen nights, Precinct Marshal Colchis Skarmen found his dreams troubled. In them, he found himself following up a spiral stair through a secret door to a shuttered chamber, where he would awake screaming at the reflection he would find in a great dark mirror there. However, one night, his nightmare became reality. He awoke to find himself standing in a dusty and cobwebbed chamber before a partly draped mirror. As if compelled, he removed its velvet covering—and looked into the eyes of the daemon.

The effort of crushing Colchis Skarmen's will and fanning the darkness in his heart was as much as the trapped daemon could do whilst still bound to the mirror. However, it now had a servant in the material world and a means of finding the shards of the second mirror to break free of its prison. Many of these pieces had been taken by Sinophia Magna's criminals and nobles and changed hands numerous times over the years, for the mirror shards were wondrous things that could show incredible sights to those who gazed into them. The daemon was linked to the shards, which contained slivers of its slumbering warp-spawned power, but it could not sense or influence them directly thanks to its imprisonment. To recover them purely through guile and in secrecy would require time that the daemon did not have, as it knew that the powers that had awoken it meant only one thing—Haarlock was returning.

Forced into direct action (but hamstrung by its prison and left vulnerable), the daemon has mangled Skarmen's soul with whispers of sorcery and revenge against those on Sinophia who had long defied judgement in order to carry out its plans. The daemon used the half-corrupted, half-enslaved Precinct Marshal as its eyes and hands, using the Arbiters' own data-cores in conjunction with its own half-blinded, esoteric senses to isolate and track down the remaining shards or those who might have knowledge of them. As the shards were slowly uncovered, it used Skarmen to create a force of animate dead from the corpses held in the Arbites Precinct mortuaries. With these risen cadavers, it began secretly hunting down those who might have fragments of the second mirror. Such brutal methods risked discovery of its thrall, but the daemon counted on the paranoia and suspicion of the Sinophians to look for easier answers as to the agency behind the attacks. So far, it has not been disappointed. However, as the plot has progressed, the daemon has grown ever more impatient and the attacks have grown bloodier. The rapidly worsening situation on Sinophia has drawn the attention, however reluctantly and belatedly, of the Holy Ordos of the Inquisition. Worse still for the daemon's plans, the remaining targets are no easy marks, and even more bloody measures may soon be called for by an increasingly unstable Skarmen. The daemon thirsts for freedom and cares nothing for the consequences, for it is aware that time is running out.

KEY DRAMATIS PERSONAE

The following section details some of the key personalities and motivations of important NPCs in DAMNED CITIES. As with the Adventure Background and the Sinophia Gazetteer, these key personalities are covered here in considerable detail so that the GM can use them to elaborate further encounters, intrigues, and events for the adventure as he sees fit.

FIHAD CONSTANTINE— ARBITRATOR ADJUTANT

Fihad Constantine is a young and idealistic Arbitrator whose family hails from the far and dread Mandragora Sector, a factor enough on its own for some to consider him suspect and has resulted to his posting to Sinophia after it became known to his last commander. Constantine has not been long on Sinophia, having been only recently posted to the blighted world. He was not part of the planet's Arbiter force the night that Haarlock's Folly came alive and had not been long in Sinophia Magna when the attacks and murders first began. Ever mindful of the teachings of vigilance instilled into all Arbitrators, Constantine sees the malign possibilities in the attacks and has ensured that reports of what is occurring have gotten off-world, and it is actually his diligence that has alerted the Holy Ordos to the murders.

Raised in the Schola Progenium, Constantine is about as naive as any trained to enforce the Emperor's law can be, despite being physically brave, loyal, and faithful. His chief weakness is that his suspicion does not naturally extend to his superiors or those who should share his duty. Surprisingly strong willed, he has yet to fall to the mind-clouding effects of Skarmen's sorcery. He does not suspect that the Precinct Marshal, a man he has great respect for (although he considers him somewhat worn out by his duties), may be at the centre of what is occurring. Constantine welcomes the Acolytes as servants of the Golden Throne and (almost alone of those they encounter) offers whatever aid he can freely give—he is their closest potential ally.

THE DAEMON IN THE MIRROR

The daemon that Haarlock bound is a powerful warp entity of great knowledge and infinite malice that has spun lies and misery for countless ages that cannot be measured in terms understood by mortals. No mindless predator of the warp, its chief power and domain is knowledge of the possible and potential end of things that are hidden to the linear perceptions of those bound by realspace. These hollow secrets have tempted mortals to ruin and garnered many souls in the daemon's long and unnatural existence. It has been known by countless names and titles over the years, and obscure references can be found to it in Sinophian lore going back to the world's founding as both the Shade of Misrule and the Beggar of Truth. Its true name is known only to Erasmus Haarlock and to itself. Here and now, to Skarmen and those it has touched, it is simply known as the Mirror Daemon.

The daemon woefully underestimated Erasmus Haarlock, considering him a "mere mortal." Haarlock tricked and bound the daemon, and forced it to answer Haarlock's questions about events that may be undone. The daemon was paid in torment when its answers failed to please him. The daemon fears him almost as much as it hates him and is desperate to be free before Haarlock, or more accurately the thing it fears Haarlock has become, returns from the outer void. Therefore, escape is the dominant motivation for the daemon in the mirror, and it uses any means and tools it can to achieve its ends. Its direct power is sharply curtailed by its capturing glass, but in its agent Colchis Skarmen it has invested its will, and via the lore of whispered sorceries it has been able (through him) to create other servants to aid its escape. Given its nature, it would also be willing to exchange its freedom for knowledge; particularly, it gladly gives up knowledge that might hurt Erasmus Haarlock—should anyone in a position to set it free desire such knowledge, that is. Should it break free, its instinct is (perhaps surprisingly) not be to linger and wreak havoc on Sinophia, but to make good its escape back to the depths of the warp, pausing only to lash out at any to hand that tries to prevent its escape.

COLCHIS SKARMEN—SENIOR ADEPTUS ARBITES PRECINCT MARSHAL

Colchis Skarmen was once a loyal, hard-working, and experienced Arbites Officer in his late middle years (who would have risen higher in the ranks of the Adeptus Arbites were it not for some long-distant slight or political mistake) which has meant that his career has been one of blighted mediocrity. His recent posting to Sinophia Magna as Precinct Marshal and nominal head of the Adeptus Arbites on the planet occurred after his predecessor's death in the Empty Men incident. It should have been considered an honourable promotion, were it not for Sinophia's status as an outcast backwater and dumping ground for unwanted members of the Adepta. Despite the ignominy of his posting, the galling disregard the Sinophians hold his office, the ingrained criminality of the planet's society, and the endless petty machinations, slights, and indignities heaped upon the Adeptus Arbites by the local authorities, Precinct Marshal Skarmen has for more than a year persevered and attended to his duties with care and diligence.

All this changed from the moment Colchis Skarmen found the mirror and stared into the daemon reflection looking back at him. From this moment, the old Skarmen was no more; his will was broken, and his slumbering hatred and prejudices were fanned white hot. He became the Mirror Daemon's physical agent in its plan to escape from its prison. Colchis Skarmen is effectively the daemon's will bound in flesh and has been using sorcery and warp-craft to create enslaved killers from the corpses of the dead. He wields his influence as Precinct Marshal to conceal the true nature of the crimes he himself has initiated and to exacerbate the dangerously unstable situation in Sinophia Magna. Skarmen, however, is becoming increasingly unstable and volatile in response to the steady corruption of his body and soul.

Skarmen's chief concern is discovering and retrieving the thirteen shards of the broken mirror to free the daemon, whilst keeping knowledge of what he is doing from others—most especially his subordinates in the Arbites. In return, the daemon has promised him the power to revenge himself on the whole corrupt edifice of Sinophia and those who have long slighted him. In his task, he has been aided by his ruling daemon's cunning. He has occasionally risked the use of sorcery to cloud the minds of those Arbiters directly under his command who might question his judgement or inquire why the Precinct Marshal spends so long in the mortuary…

SKARMEN AND THE ACOLYTES

Skarmen is, of course, the villain of the piece, as the Acolytes should eventually discover. He hides this fact as long as he can under a veil of careful misdirection, inertia, plausibly thrown blame, and the persona of an embittered enforcer of the law, whose "hands are tied" more than he would wish.

Skarmen's reaction to the Acolytes' investigation is one of grudging cooperation and civil, if somewhat strained, deference. However, he always shows proper respect for the authority of the Inquisition, at least to their faces. If asked for his personal opinion, he offers that (in his judgement) they are on Sinophia on a empty errand, and that the murders are merely more savagery on the part of the nobility and the Undertow. He regards both as recidivists and unworthy to live but shielded from judgment so long as they do not contravene the writ Imperial Law.

XIABIUS KHAN—ENFORCER GENERAL

Xiabius Khan is the Enforcer General in charge of the Sanctum Enforcers, Sinophia's infamous and brutal local law enforcement agency. He is a former off-world bounty hunter

who plied his trade across the Malfian Subsector for three decades and has now manoeuvred himself into a position as the pet monster of the dissolute Sinophian nobility. As Enforcer General, Khan reports directly to the Quorum and the Judiciary—who imbues him with his authority and finances him and the Sanctum Enforcers. The sole concern of Khan's masters is the maintenance of their power and position, a desire that grows all the more keen with every step that Sinophia takes into ruin. As a result, Khan is given license to indulge any viciousness or personal avarice he pleases as long as he keeps the rotting elite in power. Khan is a ruthless and sinister individual who has built an organisation of cruel, sadistic men and women beneath him and wields them like a weapon. Privately, he has long harboured the ambition to take over dominance of the Sinophia Magna's criminal trade from the Undertow, but despite the power behind him, he is enough of a realist to know that he would likely die in an open conflict with them.

Chief amongst the monsters who serve Xiabius Khan are the Mandato; a secret police force made up of torturers, assassins, and worse who report to Khan personally. With members of the nobility being brutally murdered, Khan has become personally convinced that the Undertow are sending him a message to stop him from trying to muscle in on their territory. He is in no mood to give in to their pressure, but at the same time is torn between his fears: that should he not smash the Undertow, he will be removed by the Quorum and cast to his many enemies, or that his fears of the wrath of the Undertow roused against him are indeed true.

Khan is well aware of the Acolytes' arrival on Sinophia and is keeping a discreet watch on them during their stay. As long as they avoid meddling too closely in his business and that of those he serves, he is more than willing to let them sink or swim alone. If they prove more troublesome, however, a suitably untraceable accident can be arranged. It wouldn't be the first time he's played such a game with Inquisition operatives at a safe distance.

Khan also possesses a fragment of the mirror sought by the daemon, set into a medallion of honour bestowed on him by the Judiciary of Sinophia; a fact that will likely prove fatal to the Enforcer General as matters progress.

MARGRAVE CAL SUR'MAYWROTH— MALEVOLENT NOBLE

Leader of the House of Maywroth, Cal (the prefix 'Sur' on Sinophia indicates his status as the familial patriarch, whilst Margrave is his title of ennoblement) is a whip-thin elderly man with silvered augmetics keeping him mobile despite his advanced age and the ravages of a dissolute lifestyle. Considered something of a treacherous villain even by his peers on the Quorum, Cal sees the unfolding events as an opportunity to advance his increasingly poverty-stricken and struggling house. He is also one of the loudest proponents in the Quorum demanding that the Undertow (or the "drowned lickspittles" as he calls them) be taught a final lesson about

who rules Sinophia—up to and including the use of nerve gas on the slums and wholesale executions and block burnings.

Cal affects a superior air and is faultlessly polite to those he considers worthy of his attention, but at the same time there is an almost starving hunger to the man and something entirely unwholesome in his glittering black eyes, perfect ivory teeth, and the faint reek of rot beneath his perfume.

Cal is not directly involved with the shards of the mirror, but as a vociferous proponent of open conflict he and his house represent an obvious target of choice for the Undertow. He happily uses hired agents of his own in 'revenge' attacks against the Undertow, thus worsening matters. Additionally, if the Acolytes are drawn to investigate the nobility's role in the conflict, Cal is an obvious NPC port of call and he is more likely than not to try and bribe or suborn them to his own ends.

THE SAGACITY EUPHEME TASSEL— KEEPER OF THE ROLLS

Eupheme Tassel is a minor noblewoman barely in her thirties who inherited the hereditary position of Keeper of the Rolls some years ago on the death of her father and grandfather— 'the Sagacity' is a seemingly ill-fitting honorific associated with the position. As Keeper of the Rolls, she is nominally in charge of the Quorum's heavily edited official records of government. However, in practice, this is managed by a faceless morass of grey adepts and withered lexicographic servitors, and she has very little to do except sit it her official chambers in the Clockwork Court. There, she expends her time stamping her seal on archives occasionally, slowly cracking the ciphers on her grandfather's private archives, dabbling in the fragments of forbidden lore she has found there, and passing the evenings with pinches of Night Dust.

Eupheme is withdrawn and sullen, but she is also well aware of her rank and station and is not afraid to act every inch the aristocrat when she needs to. She is also far more intelligent than she lets on and has—thanks to her privileged position— absorbed much of Sinophia's history, myth, and politics (both real and fabricated). As a result, she can potentially provide a wealth of information the Acolytes can use on the city, and its past, the factions, and what's going on.

A large shard of the broken mirror rests in a lacquerwood box forgotten on a shelf in the Keeper's chambers. This shard was used by her grandfather as a scrying device, but its presence is quite unknown to Eupheme—unfortunately for her chances of survival.

THE MASTERS OF THE UNDERTOW— HESUL, TIBER, AND SCORN

Criminality in Sinophia Magna and its environs is controlled by the Undertow, a pervasive and organized confederation of smugglers, scrap gleaners, raconteurs, extortionists, robbers, murderers, and thieves. The Undertow itself is ruled at any one time by powerful underworld bosses called Rag-Kings and Queens. Three of the most powerful of these make up the Rag Court, a ruling council which maintains the peace between rival factions of the Undertow, decides policy, and metes out punishment to those who cross the organisation. The current Rag Court is made up of Hesul, Tiber, and Scorn.

Without exception, the Rag Court dislikes and distrusts each other. Indeed, past conflicts have led to bloodshed between the vassals of the Rag-Kings. The Rag Court has recently been shaken by the death of one of its own and a number of senior members of the Undertow. Mutterings and rumours lay the blame either with a group of disaffected nobles, or that these deaths are the beginning of an attempt by Enforcer General Khan to take over their criminal empire for himself. Their differences for the time forgotten in the face of possible extinction, the Rag Court is willing to preserve its criminal empire at any cost, including large scale bloodshed. It has the arms and manpower to pose a very serious threat to Sinophia's rulers if its members have the will to do so.

HESUL

Hesul was raised in the slums of Sinophia Magna's District XIII and has since fought her way up to control the Undertow baronies of the southern city. A former torturer for hire and assassin, she has the darkest reputation of any of the Rag-Queens and serves as the Rag Court's chief enforcer. Also known as Red, some whisper she is a witch in league with daemons; this is untrue, she is merely evil, cold-blooded, and inventively sadistic in a way most people can barely begin to imagine. Alone among the Rag Court, Hesul harbours serious doubts about the murders and whether the nobility or the Enforcers are truly to blame. She has her own trusted agents and intermediaries looking into the matter covertly, agents whose paths are likely to cross with the Acolytes in turn.

TIBER

A great blustering slab of muscle, Tiber controls much of the Undertow's 'meat work,' including providing muscle for off-world smuggling operations, running labour rackets, and canal piracy in the city. He has only just come to the Rag Court after the brutal murder of Callisto, his former boss, who previously held one of the three ruling seats. Tiber is loudest among the Rag-Kings in his calls for vengeance against the nobles and has done little to quell the mutterings of armed revolt in the ranks of those beneath him.

Scorn

The nominal head of the Rag Court, Scorn is a bloated and grasping old man who has the major control of narcotic production and distribution on Sinophia, but whose real power is as the principle banker to the Undertow. He also holds debt markers for a surprising number of dissolute noble houses in secret, and is able to manipulate them accordingly. Scorn is perplexed and confused by the turn of events, and though enraged by what he sees as a betrayal and the nobility overstepping their bounds, he has little stomach for revolt, knowing it will ultimately bring the Imperium's wrath down on Sinophia again. He also has the most to lose from an all-out conflict, and he knows it. Scorn has done much to hold back the Undertow from open reprisals (so far), but should matters worsen, he throws in his lot for war—at least until more tractable nobles can be found to replace the dead ones. Then, the two factions can present a façade of normality to the wider Imperium so they can get back to business as usual.

If he can be somehow approached and convinced that some other agency (such as Marshal Skarmen) is really to blame (and the problem can be made to go away), he gladly offers bribery and such assistance as he believes he can get away with—as long as it can't be traced back to him, particularly if the death of Arbites officers is involved, no matter how corrupted they may be.

LYNAN YANTRA— THE WITNESS

Yantra is an ordinary man caught up in terrible events beyond his ability to comprehend or control. Although this makes him but one of many, Yantra is singular in that he is one of the few surviving witnesses to the attacks of Skarmen's Risen. Sheltering in the same chop-house as the murdered dreg Sokken when the Risen came for him (see page 46), Yantra is now on the run, justly fearing for his life because of what he has seen—but without money or friends, he is going nowhere quickly. If the Acolytes get wind of him, they are not the only ones on his trail, as both the Undertow and Skarmen's Risen are looking for him.

Although a relatively young man, Yantra's drifting life spent heating scrap for semi-precious metals and other toxic pursuits have prematurely aged him and left him with grey, blood-speckled skin and an asthmatic rasp when he exerts himself. All he wants is to be safe, and any who can offer him that will learn all he knows without hesitation.

BIOLOGIS-ADEPT LECTO TALANIS

Aged to the point of decrepitude, Talanis's useful days as a member of the Cult Mechanicus are long since passed, with his numerous implants and augmetics failing and tarnished, barely supported by his withered organic components. Assigned to assist the Arbites Precinct as medical examiner because the local Machine Cult considers him expendable, much of what made Talanis a sentient creature capable of independent thought was dead long before Skarmen's sorcery corrupted it into serving the daemon.

Talanis's personality can be summed up in a single word: empty. Devoid utterly of purpose, he carries out his duties as instructed and defend his master's secrets to the death without knowing or caring why.

(OPTIONAL) SPECTRE CELL 17—TENEBRAE COLLEGIUM KILL TEAM

In the case of very experienced Acolyte teams playing this adventure, ones with considerable resources at their disposal, or who have already experienced the other adventures of the Haarlock Legacy up to this point, GMs may wish to add another, potentially lethal faction into this adventure in the shape of Spectre Cell 17.

The Spectre Cells are hand-picked Inquisitorial kill-teams that serve the hidden Tenebrae Collegium, the ultra-secret conspiracy at the heart of the Tyrantine Cabal. The Tenebrae Collegium is dedicated to gathering dangerous knowledge of the Tyrant Star into its own hands and preventing it from being discovered by others who might misuse it—which, as far as many within the Collegium are concerned, is just about anybody, including rivals within the Inquisition. The Spectre Cells are small teams of combat-oriented and highly indoctrinated Acolytes who are used by the secret masters of the Collegium to clean up any circumstances that could lead to dangerous knowledge or artefacts passing into the hands of others in extremis. In unleashing such a cell, the primary intent of the Collegium is to remove rivals and witnesses with deadly force.

Spectre Cell 17 is made up of four highly trained and ruthlessly efficient operatives who are all products of the Collegium's training programs that produce unbreakable secret operatives. Spectre Cell 17 has been sent to Sinophia to shadow the Acolytes; they are here in secret because the murders conform to certain patterns that have troubled the Collegium in the past. There are also those in the Collegium who suspect that Erasmus Haarlock, should the connection be known or guessed, possessed dangerous knowledge of the Tyrantine Star and Propheticum Hereticus Tenebrae which the Acolytes may discover. If the Acolytes have already taken part in the dark events depicted in either The House of Dust and Ash or TATTERED FATES, they may already know too much.

Cell 17 has been tasked with first observing, then if necessary, eliminating the Acolytes and anyone else who may be involved with the Collegium's concern. In pursuit of these goals they will not be deterred, although they may wish to surreptitiously aid the Acolytes whilst their investigations are progressing if it serves their ultimate ends. Bound by oath and cerebral conditioning, the members of Spectre Cell 17 cannot be turned, bribed, or bargained with, though they may engage in discussion with the Acolytes to discover what they know before executing them.

The individual members of this team are dealt with in the NPCs and Antagonists chapter on page 58.

THE SHATTERED MIRROR

The thirteen fragments of shattered mirror together make up the whole, and if re-assembled facing its twin, the artefact will free the daemon trapped there by Erasmus Haarlock. These thirteen fragments were taken from Haarlock's Folly after the disappearance of Haarlock himself when the tower was looted at the behest of the Sinophian nobility. Valued for the "wondrous things they reflect," these warp-touched fragments have changed hands amongst the criminal class and dissolute aristocracy of Sinophia for many years, and in some cases they are now merely regarded as precious and rare objects. Others treat them rightly as blasphemous artefacts, and hide them away from prying eyes.

WHO HAS THE MIRROR FRAGMENTS?

Recovering the fragments from their many owners is Precinct Marshal Skarmen's goal. Those who held the thirteen fragments at the beginning of **DAMNED CITIES** are as follows, starting with those who have already been murdered for their shards in the order their killings occurred:

PREVIOUS VICTIMS

Callisto (murdered): A Rag-King of the Undertow, Callisto claimed his shard showed him the truth when he looked into it. This rumour, widely known in underworld circles, meant that he was the first target Skarmen had eliminated in what appeared to be a simple if very messy assassination.

Mam'sel Zamura Rolart (murdered): A famed, painted beauty belonging to a minor but well-connected noble house, she was known to boast when drunk that she had "a thing that old Haarlock himself was proud to look on." In fact, the small mirror fragment was set into a gaudy ring given to her by a would-be suitor. She was torn apart at her dressing table when Skarmen learnt of her claim; the room was ransacked to look like a more general robbery.

Legate Senh-Ar Dole (murdered): An off-world trader belonging to neither nobility nor the Undertow, Dole was also a prominent private money lender to whom half of the Sinophian nobility were said to be indebted. Unknown to most, he had accepted a fragment of Haarlock's mirror set as part of a diadem as a guarantee on a loan that was never repaid. The debtor was first tracked down and made to disappear; then Dole and his entire household were murdered for the prize. Sinophia did not mourn his passing, but the chaos caused by the disposition of his estate and the numerous promissory notes owed to him had serious repercussions among the nobility.

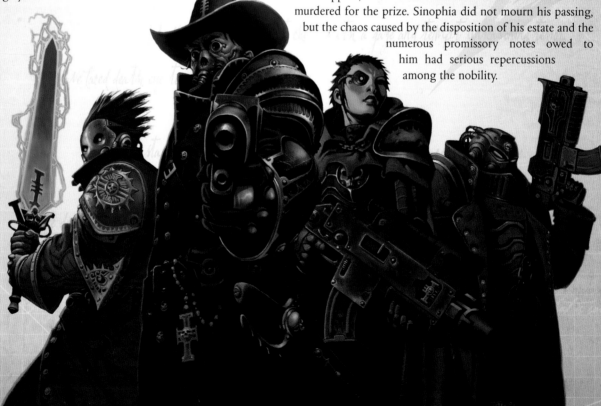

Viscount Hiram Sur'Seculo (murdered): A grandee of a noble merchant house with a seat on the Quorum. Skarmen learnt of the prized "seeing glass" that the master would show off to favoured guests behind closed doors and had him killed to recover it, breaking into the noble's villa in the night and slaughtering all the family and servants to cover up the true nature of the crime. Generally regarded as a "revenge killing" by the Undertow for the deaths of Callisto after Skarmen covertly spread rumours to this effect, this killing sparked off the great rise in tensions between the underworld and the nobility.

Juvinal Priator (murdered): An Undertow slaver and lesser Rag-King with a taste for the forbidden and blasphemous, Priator had acquired two fragments of mirror from an 'acquaintance' in full knowledge that they were dangerous artefacts stolen from the Folly and said to foretell the future. One he kept for himself; the other was offered to end a feud with fellow criminal Bal Grey following a botched obscura deal. Before he died, he pleaded with the Risen that he could get the other fragment from "Bal" and so sealed the fate of Bal Grey as well as his own.

Priator's death has gone unreported to the authorities, and his body still lies in his hideout (See The Late Juvinal Priator encounter description on page 44)

Sokken (murdered): Considered by most no more than a mad dreg, the man known as Sokken was once an ordinary hab-worker when he discovered a mirror fragment floating in a canal mire. Driven insane by the visions he saw within, he lost everything and took to wandering the streets muttering and ranting, prey to Magna's dreadful elements. He survived and never relinquished his grip on the fragment, only to be eventually found and killed by Skarmen's Risen as he sheltered in a chop-shop. Skarmen bungled a cover-up of the murder, and a single witness, Lynan Yantra, lived to tell of the attack. (See the On the Run encounter on page 46).

Bal Grey (murdered): Skarmen learnt that Grey, a minor Undertow boss, had been paid off with a "sliver of scrying mirror" to end a gang feud and finally succeeded in tracking down the PDF veteran to his hideout. Grey was murdered there and his mirror fragment retrieved hours before the Acolytes arrive on Sinophia (see The Corpse of Bal Grey encounter description on page 40).

Colchis Skarmen: Skarmen happened upon a fragment of the mirror, the last left in the chamber that would become his office while setting up the folly as the Arbites base, thinking little of the discovery, but keeping it nevertheless—an act which was to doom him on the night of the storm and provide a link through which the malice of the daemon could flow at such proximity.

Skarmen's Next Planned Targets

Lady Amorite: A grand old matriarch of Sinophia Magna who has not stirred beyond the shuttered rooms of her fortified manse for decades. Within, she rots, attended by servitors and servants and wrapped in dusty lace, gazing into a jagged-edged mirror in which she sees her lost beauty again (see The House of Amorite encounter description on page 50).

Judiciary Evandus Idrani: The ruler of Sinophia Magna, at least in title, this jaded fop has a fragment of mirror set in a silver hand frame which he likes to carry around to admire his complexion. His vanity may cost him his life (see the Death in the Clockwork Court encounter on page 46). Should the Judiciary die, tensions on Sinophia explode into outright violence. A bloodbath likely ensues as the Enforcers, spurred on by a panicking nobility, attempt a violent crackdown and the Undertow responds in kind.

Eupheme Tassel: The somewhat dissolute hereditary Keeper of the Rolls at the Clockwork Court, she is unaware that a fragment of the mirror is among her late grandfather's effects in her court chambers. Tassel is a potential ally for the Acolytes and can offer considerable insight into the events and history of Sinophia (See the Unvarnished Truth encounter on page 50), if bribed or suborned into doing so. Tassel's mirror is either stolen during the attack on the Clockwork Court or given to the Acolytes, marking them as targets in turn.

Enforcer General Xiabius Khan: The brutal master of the Enforcers has a small fragment of mirror worked into a medallion of honour. Of all the remaining carriers of the mirror, he is the best prepared to defend himself with an army of trained killers at his beck and call, and he is the last target on Skarmen's list. However, no one is truly safe from an unseen and unknown foe.

Rumours in Sinophia Magna

Sinophia Magna is rife with rumours, and even a brief time in the city will expose an Acolyte to one or other of them. The GM should invent and spin rumours to fit the circumstance, but selections are presented in each State of Turmoil entry for more specific applications. Some are utterly false, some have distorted undercurrents of truth, and some are absolutely on the money—not that many of the people saying them know that for a fact!

- *"The Quorum has been taken over by House Krin minions with over half the council in the pay of off-worlders."*
- *"The Imperial military has secret bases on the planet to stockpile bio-weapons."*
- *"There have been two attempts in the last week by kill squads to eliminate two prominent Rag-Kings."*
- *"The Enforcer General has secretly taken psykers into the Mandato; they are going to know what we are thinking!"*
- *"Three people have died in the last week in horrible circumstances that defy imagination—apparently the last fellow ripped himself apart, and the Adeptus Arbites are trying to cover it up."*
- *"People keep hearing screaming around the Cathedral at night."*
- *"The world has been selected as an outer base for Battlefleet Calixis—Sinophia is going to enjoy the golden times again."*
- *"Several Quorum families have had their markers bought by the dreaded Iron Eye Syndicate; and they only way they can pay up now is to sell their workers into slavery."*
- *"People have seen lights around the old haunted tower out on the headland. Perhaps doom has come to us all!"*

The Last Fragment: Who has the last fragment, its location, and to which faction the owner (if any) belongs to has been left up to the GM to decide—although he is also at liberty to change any of the above as well! If the GM doesn't wish to do this, however, it can simply be assumed that this fragment is already in Skarmen's possession and that the murder needed to claim it has gone completely unknown.

THE NATURE OF THE SHARD FRAGMENTS

Erasmus Haarlock's twin mirrors were made to foul, alchemical specifications using forbidden methods and materials twisted by his own genius. Each mirror fragment is also corrupted by the shredded essence of the daemon whose consciousness is bound within the shattered mirror's twin. Outwardly, the fragments appear like utterly mundane pieces of a broken mirror, ranging from small chips fashioned into the settings of jewellery since their theft, or larger chunks and jagged shards. Close inspection reveals them to be perfectly reflective and, other than their broken edges, utterly without mark or blemish.

Any Acolyte with the Psyniscience Skill senses that a powerful psychic emanation from a fragment. A successful **Easy (+20) Psyniscience** or **Ordinary (+10) Forbidden Lore (Daemonology) Skill Test** reveals that the energy of the warp permeates the fragment but that it also is bound into it in some way. Another potentially shocking discovery is that they appear to be indestructible to any force applied to them. Further inspection with an auspex set up to monitor Geller fields and similar effects reveals that somehow they are in some way out of phase with reality and not wholly within realspace.

LOOKING INTO THE MIRROR

Whilst the Game Master should feel free to alter the effects of looking into the mirror fragments, Table 2–1 below should serve as a guideline as to what may be seen when looking into their reflective surfaces, noting that since the daemon's awakening, the mirrored fragments are somewhat more active than previously.

TABLE 2-1: STARING INTO THE GLASS

Roll 1d100 whenever an Acolyte looks into a fragment on mirror. Once someone looks into a mirror fragment and receives a vision, that is the same vision they see every time they look into it. Often, the vision is tailored specifically to that individual's personality, desires, and fears. Looking into the mirror more than once is dangerous. Each time someone looks into the mirror and does not see a vision (i.e., gains a result of 61 or higher), the next time he looks he will add +20 to the roll. The GM should feel free to alter the description of the vision to match something particularly significant to the character who is looking into the mirror.

Roll	Result
01–20	Nothing happens, the mirror reflects as normal.
21-60	The viewer passes several minutes in reverie unless roused by others and is completely unaware of the passage of time, entranced by the reflected light in the glass.
61-80	The mirror reflects a normal image but one so perfect and clear that it is as if the fragment is a jagged window through which someone identical to the viewer looks back. A tearing sense of dislocation accompanies any attempt to look away from this reflection, as if the viewer has left some part of himself behind. The character gains 1 Insanity Point.
80-90	The fragment holds a brief glimpse of some faraway place, past or future close to the viewer's heart for a brief second before darkness overwhelms the image.
91-95	The viewer sees a terrible gaunt face with burning dark eyes raising his hand to strike toward the viewer, who flinches as if the blow connects and pains something deep inside him. (If the viewer has seen his portrait, they will recognise this as an image of Erasmus Haarlock.) The viewer gains 1 Corruption Point.
96-00	Something terrible lurks in the glass; roll for Psychic Phenomena (see page 162 of **DARK HERESY**).

THE BLOODY TIDE OF DISORDER

"No matter how established, how stable or how pious, every fragmented part of our Imperium is separated from terror and anarchy by naught but a shadow's width. And where one world falls, another may follow over the edge of the abyss as a drowning man might take another down with him in his desperate grasp."

—attributed to Sebastian Thor

DAMNED **CITIES** is an adventure of mystery and horror set against the dark background of a city that is sliding from fear into calamity and bloodshed. As events progress, the nature of the city, its character, and the disposition of its citizens should change as the Acolytes interact with the city, just as Sinophia Magna's general atmosphere of tension and mistrust slowly breaks down into fear-fuelled violence and disorder. Eventually, if the Acolytes through their investigations cannot avert it, the rising tide of repercussion and terror overwhelm the city, and Sinophia Magna erupts into all-out bloody civil war.

The Acolytes' actions may affect this slide into calamity either directly or indirectly, or shift its focus and emphasis. The changing mood of Sinophia Magna is primarily a means of injecting a sense of increasing danger and urgency into the adventure.

THE STATE OF TURMOIL

The changing mood and antipathy of Sinophia and its population is represented by the city's State of Turmoil. This mechanic outlines the general mindset of the population, the level of danger and violence, and the sights and sounds of the city. As events progress, the city changes from one State of Turmoil to another. The GM has ultimate control of these transitions and should base them on how things unfold during play. A number of key trigger events are suggested that should spur an increase in the tension.

Each of the adventure's three parts has its own suggested State of Turmoil and trigger events which may cause things to worsen or improve, if the Acolytes can help stabilise things in the city. Some suggested rumours and responses are appropriate to them. As a GM, keeping track of both the State of Turmoil and what each of the factions and parties involved are doing in response is crucial to maintaining the dynamic sense of changing events. The GM should feel free to change the amount of time that occurs between each State of Turmoil: If the players need a greater sense of urgency, then make the time between each transition shorter to create a sense of pressure and events rapidly spiralling out of control. If the players are missing important details and rushing too much, then the GM may decide to allow the State of Turmoil

to rise more slowly, creating a sense of unfolding doom.

Each of the states of turmoil corresponds broadly to the three phases of the adventure:

- Rising Tension is the suggested state for most of **Part I: Death in Sinophia Magna**.
- Boiling Point is the suggested state for **Part II: Blind Enemies**.
- Mayhem is the suggested state for the climatic events of **Part III: Through the Shattered Mirror**.

Within each part of the adventure is a separate State of Turmoil section for easy reference which contains key points that the GM can use to communicate the background mood of the city to the players. These sections include a summary of what has caused the State of Turmoil, its specific effects on the Acolytes, how it affects the sights and sounds experienced by Acolytes in the city, and how the State of Turmoil affects what the citizens of Sinophia Magna may say to Acolytes.

EVENTS AND THEIR WIDER CONSEQUENCES

Whilst the Acolytes are carrying out their investigations, events continue to unfold around them as Skarmen's plan moves closer to fruition—perhaps because of their own direct intervention. If an event occurs with the power to cause significant terror to the general population or incite anger or fear in a particular faction, matters are more likely to take a turn for the worse. Several such events have been presented in the course of the adventure, such as the potential death of the Judiciary, that should (at the GM's discretion) trigger an immediate increase in the State of Turmoil, thereby beginning the next phase of the adventure and furthering Magna's slid into anarchy.

If the Acolytes succeed in stopping such trigger events from happening, or perhaps succeed in mollifying the faction leaders (or at least casting a shadow of doubt over their suspicions) by presenting them with evidence that suggest other powers are involved in the murders, they can attempt to stabilise the situation in the city.

Although it's not realistic to expect a single foiled murder to return Magna to a state of normality, the Acolytes can make a difference by convincing those capable of maintaining order in the Quorum, the Enforcers, and the Undertow that they should hold off from a conflict that will assuredly harm themselves as well as their enemies. Just how they do this, and whether Skarmen can stop them, is in the hands of the Acolytes.

ADVENTURE PROLOGUE

The Acolytes arrive in Sinophia and begin the adventure either because of their past involvement with the dark affair of the Haarlock Legacy, or as the beginning of their unwitting entanglement with the Rogue Trader's inheritance. In either case, the Acolytes have been sent by the Holy Ordos to investigate the mysterious spate of murders in Sinophia. The resultant unrest from these murders threatens to destabilise an entire Imperial world.

DEATH BEGETS DISCORD, DISCORD BEGETS HERESY

If the Acolytes have no prior connection with the Haarlock Legacy, either because this is adventure is being run as the first in the sequence or on its own, they have been diverted to investigate the troubling events on Sinophia Magna simply because they are the closest team their Inquisitor and their allies in the Ordos have. They have been diverted from a supporting role in an ongoing clean-up operation following a purge there.

In this circumstance, the adventure begins for the players with a briefing on board the merchant scow *Tarsus's Pride*. The GM should expound upon Sinophia's dissolute status as a past lightning-rod of heresy, and that what happens there could ultimately have repercussions for nearby worlds if the past is any indicator. In such cases, a conspiracy exposed and purged now could well prevent taint spread unseen to more valuable worlds.

HAARLOCK CONNECTION

If the Acolytes are embroiled in the Haarlock Legacy, they are coming to Sinophia Magna because their masters in the Inquisition have learned of baleful occurrences on Sinophia, a world known in the sealed archives of the Tricorn Palace as also possessing former domains belonging to the Haarlock bloodline. This fact is simply too much of a coincidence for those interested in the Legacy to ignore, and so their own Inquisitor's faction, perhaps at the request of Lord Inquisitor Marr (see The House of Dust and Ash), has made sure that the Acolytes are the ones who receive the task of the investigation—giving them, in effect, a double-agenda to both uncover the heresy and learn what they can about any connection to the events of the Legacy. In this case, they are diverted from a cover mission on Cyclopea to Sinophia, a fact that should lead astute Acolytes to deduce that the Haarlock angle to the affair is being concealed from others in the Inquisition itself...

The Acolytes receive a communiqué via regular channels from their own Inquisitor or another they have done recent work for (see Appendix II: Player Handout on page 67).

A SUDDEN CHANGE OF ORDERS

Midway to the world of Cyclopea to act in support of an ongoing purge there, the Acolytes receive new orders to deal with a situation that has arisen on the world of Sinophia.

Read or paraphrase the following:

> *Your journey to an unremarkable deployment of Inquisitorial forces on the world of Cyclopea has been cut short by a priority astropathic communication. Your vessel, the merchant scow* Tarsus's Pride, *has been diverted to the ill-reputed world of Sinophia. For hours now, the battered old vessel as been preparing itself for acceleration and course change, the bleak-eyed captain muttering at the risk your masters have forced on him and that no good comes of travel to this blighted world. The other passengers of this scheduled flight have taken to shying away from you with a mixture of fear and resentment. It comes as something of a relief when at last you retire to your secure quarters to prepare for the warp transit and open your sealed, encrypted orders.*

The Acolytes' orders contain a copy of an astropathic communiqué describing details of a series of murders in the city of Sinophia Magna and a missive from the Acolytes' Inquisitor ordering them to investigate, uncover any corruption, and purge it from the domain of the God-Emperor. Give the players Player Handout I (see page 67). The *Tarsus's Pride* takes two weeks to reach Sinophia at its best speed during a somewhat troubled journey, as the old ship is tested to its limits. On the ship's arrival, the Acolytes deploy to the surface without delay. Afterwards, the captain departs, having discharged his duty, at which point it is time for the Acolytes to enter the damned cities and confront the nightmare that lurks beneath its surface.

```
CLASSIFICATION: Void/Void/Void/
DATE: ERROR
SUBJECT: Ref: Recent Occurrences in
Sinophia Magna

++The Sinophian Matter is More than it
Appears ++That Dark-hearted Haarlock
made a home here before he disappeared
++My sources reports that strange lights
were reported at his 'Folly' at almost
the same time as @~~~@error@~~@ and I'm
sure you remember what a lovely mess that
turned into ++And now 'unnatural' murder,
a city on the brink of destruction,
it all sounds too familiar to be co-
incidence doesn't it? ++Well enough, I
am sick of being in the dark, waiting for
another atrocity to happen++ We must know
what is going on and why, we have larger
fears to content with here ++Investigate
these murders, but Sinophia be damned,
find out what the Haarlock connection is,
what it portends at any and all costs
++Go with my Blessing and My Command++
Marr++
```

Part I: Death in Sinophia Magna

The first part of the adventure proper deals with the Acolytes' arrival on Sinophia and initial investigations into the mysterious and troubling events there.

State of Turmoil for Part I—Rising Tension

When the Acolytes begin **Damned Cities**, Sinophia Magna is in a state of rising tension caused by the recent murders of members of the nobility and Undertow. The anticipation of an impending open war between the criminal underworld and the Enforcers who serve the nobility is palpable.

The murder of members of the nobility and Undertow has caused both sides to believe that the other is making a serious bid to take over or destroy them. This, in turn, has caused the general population to become worried and distrustful.

Game Effects

Members of the general population are distrustful of strangers. Unless stated otherwise, all Interaction Tests using Charm, Command, or Deceive suffer a −10 modifier; when using the guidelines for Dispositions from page 230 in **Chapter VIII: The Game Master** of **Dark Heresy** the dispositions of citizens are Disdainful, Resentful, and Suspicious respectively.

All Inquiry Tests involving members of the general population not part of the opposing factions are also made at a −10 modifier. The inherent fear of the population does, however, mean that all Intimidate Tests are made with a +20 modifier (see the Frightened disposition on Table 8–2: Dispositions in **Chapter VIII: The Game Master** of the **Dark Heresy** Rulebook).

Sights and Sounds: The rain-drenched streets of Sinophia Magna are quiet, and what few people can be seen scuttle quickly away. Passing through the streets, faces peer cautiously out from shuttered windows and doors but quickly vanish when noticed. There are few people in public places, and conversations are undertaken in hushed tones with nervous glances to see who is listening.

Rumours

- *"Three people have died in the last week in horrible circumstances that defy imagination; apparently the last ripped himself apart, and the Arbites are trying to cover it up."*
- *"People keep on seeing strange, unearthly lights around the Haarlock's Folly at night. That whole headlands is haunted and accursed."*
- *"Several noble families have had their markers bought by the dreaded Iron Eye Syndicate, and the only way they can pay up now is to sell their workers into slavery."*
- *"The enforcers are trying to crack the Undertow: there have been two attempts in the last week by kill squads to eliminate two prominent Rag-Kings."* Those closer to the Undertow express the view that they not trying to take them down, they are trying to take them over.

The Opening: A Rainy Arrival

The Acolytes arrive via atmospheric shuttle to the dilapidated Flavian Starport on the edge of Sinophia Magna (see page 14). It is dawn and raining heavily. To set the scene, read or paraphrase the following:

The small shuttle bucks and vibrates as it descends through layers of gun-grey cloud cover. Through view ports smeared with thick runnels of rain, you catch glimpses of a soaked landscape revealed in the half-light of a cloud-shrouded dawn. You are the only passengers in the cramped cargo compartment, and the door to the cockpit swings back and forth with every shudder and roll, allowing you to hear the pilot's curses and oaths. The shuttle banks sharply, sending stray equipment skittering across the floor. Through the viewports, you can glimpse the outline of a jagged-looking city of greyish green buildings the colour of corpse flesh by an iron-black sea.

With a series of jarring twists, the shuttle settles into a vertical landing on roaring thrusters, skidding in the air like a leaf on a storm wind. A sudden thump vibrates through the floor as the shuttle settles onto the ground. The pilot shouts something inaudible and the back hatch and ramp hiss open. A chill wind gusts in, and you feel the wet spray of rain on your skin. Out of the open and beckoning hatch you can see impression of low buildings beneath a solid layer of dark clouds: rain is falling in thick sheets. "Welcome to Sinophia Magna. May the Light of the Golden Throne shine on you!" sneers the voice of the pilot.

On disembarking, the Acolytes are not met by anyone, and the shuttle departs immediately after the Acolytes remove themselves from the interior. The shuttle roars off and leaves the Acolytes completely alone in a cold drizzle on a seemingly deserted landing platform atop a twenty metre rockcrete column partly covered with mildew and moss—merely one of a dozen such platforms they can see clustered around.

After a short time, a junior Administratum official called Charon makes his way out to the Acolytes; robed and hooded in grey, he is utterly soaked beneath a wide umbrella riddled with holes. Charon is quite ignorant of the Acolyte's scheduled arrival, even if details were signalled ahead, but once he knows who the Acolytes are, he is torn between fear and deference to their authority and his innate unwillingness to take responsibly

Sinophia Magna
Docks & Canals

for anything or go out of his way in the slightest.

If pressed, Charon claims that he was not expecting any craft to arrive that day and talks nervously and insistently about how few ships land craft on Sinophia these days, and things being "most irregular" and "out of my hands, you understand?" Charm or Intimidation Tests against Charon are Easy (+20) and Scrutiny Tests to discern that he is telling the complete truth are Very Easy (+30). If the Acolytes try to get information from Charon, use the Rumours in Sinophia Magna (see page 29) as a basis of what he might tell them.

GETTING INTO THE CITY

Once the Acolytes have arrived and met Charon, it is clear that there is no waited welcome for them of any kind and that the starport is little used. The city proper is approximately thirty minutes away by road, but Charon informs them that the main road itself is currently blocked by a collapsed arteria bridge. With no official welcome, the Acolytes must commandeer transport to where they want to go first in the city, and the easiest way is for them to get Charon to loan them one of the starport's motor skiffs and a pilot to take them to the city proper by water; of course, they are free to walk across the foot bridges themselves…

If the Acolytes are really determined to get some official transport, they can force Charon to get the Flavian Starport central control to communicate their presence to the Quorum, Adeptus Arbites, or both. Stating their authority gets the Acolytes an official transport waiting for them at the Commercia in Sinophia Magna, but no more. The reason given is, "All air transports are currently deployed or unavailable." The transport is either an Enforcer patrol cruiser or an Adeptus Arbites Rhino depending on whether the Acolytes requested a communiqué be sent to either the local authorities of the Arbitrators. Alternatively, Charon may suggest that the Acolytes may be able to commandeer transport into the Folly on an eight-wheeled supply wagon once they reach the city core.

OPTIONAL ENCOUNTER: DEAD IN THE WATER

The encounter presented here is suggested to occur during the Acolytes' travel to the city proper from the starport and serves as a first-hand introduction to the struggle between the city's two main factions. This encounter sees the Acolytes blundering into an attack by Undertow-backed raiders against a cargo barge belonging to House Maywroth, a noble family whose patriarch has been particularly loud in calling for blood since the murders. If the GM prefers not to have a heavy combat encounter so early in the adventure, he can either leave this encounter out entirely or have it later during another use of Magna's waterways by the Acolytes.

Read aloud or paraphrase the following:

> *Twisting and turning through the tangled waterways around a smoke-belching, thunderously noisy, and corroded manufactorum, the motor skiff rounds a junction to be confronted with a scene of ongoing battle. A rusted crane arm has crashed into the water across the canal in front of armoured cargo barge. which is now being attacked and boarded by several smaller craft, and snipers are firing down from nearby rooftops at the crew defending it. A fierce gun battle, drowned out until now by the sound of the manufactorum is, raging between the barge and its attackers, and as you watch a firebomb explodes on the barge's rear decks, sending a plume of red flame and oily smoke into the air.*

The Acolytes have the immediate option to either try to intervene in the attack, or turn tail and flee. If they dither for more than a minute or so, one of the raider motor skiffs turns and make a run at them, opening fire with a Volg crank cannon mounted on its deck (see page 121 of THE INQUISITOR'S HANDBOOK). Alternatively, the Game Master can replace this weapon with a heavy stubber from page 130 in the DARK HERESY Rulebook instead.

Successful **Challenging (+0) Perception Tests** reveal that the crew on the barge are wearing some sort of uniform (faded powder-blue flak vests) whilst their attackers are a ramshackle lot festooned in tattoos, crude cobbled-together body armour and mismatched weapons. At the GM's option, the mist and heavy rain inflicts a –10 penalty to all Ballistic Skill Tests.

There are four attacking raider skiffs, each carrying five raiders (use the Killer profile on page 65) wearing AP 2 primitive armour and carrying axes, stub automatics, and pump shotguns. Additionally, two of the skiffs have crank cannons, and the other two have boxes with a dozen firebombs each. Also, dotted in cover around the rooftops are a further four raiders armed with hunting rifles. It is suggested that the GM should abstract the portions of the combat that do not directly involve the Acolytes, reducing the amount of NPC's he needs to manage.

There are seven defenders left alive as the Acolytes arrive, four having already perished in the attack (use the Denizen's profile on page 66) wearing flak vests and carrying lasguns and clubs.

If more than half the raiders are killed or taken out of action, they flee.

Should the Acolytes give battle and prove victorious, the still somewhat suspicious crew of the barge thank them guardedly. Shortly afterward, an Enforcer air-shuttle arrives with a squad of troops.

When confronted with Inquisitorial authority, the Enforcers ask to take a statement from the Acolytes. The Enforcers treat with the Acolytes with brusque respect. The Enforcers make a show of summarily executing any prisoners on the spot and looting the bodies, deploying troops to guard the barge on its journey.

If the barge crew or the Enforcers are questioned, they happily tell their own one-sided interpretation of the current tensions in Sinophia Magna.

HAARLOCK'S FOLLY

Haarlock's Folly is a tall spire-topped tower that sits on the edge of the city of Sinophia Magna. Built by the infamous Haarlock Rogue Trader line, it has been deserted since Erasmus Haarlock disappeared. It has since been taken over by the Adeptus Arbites as a temporary headquarters following the destruction of the precinct fortress. It had previously been thoroughly looted, and its grand rooms, cellars, and internal spaces have been subject to conversion to the small Arbitrator force's basic needs.

Haarlock's Folly is at the heart of all of the mysterious events that are taking place in Sinophia Magna and appears many times during the course of the adventure. The tower fulfills many roles as events progress. Should the Acolytes begin the adventure following the trail of Haarlock's Legacy begun in adventures such as The House of Dust and Ash or **TATTERED FATES**, then Haarlock's Folly is likely one of the first locations that the Acolytes investigate, as it has the most obvious Haarlock association. Likewise, if this is their first adventure within the Haarlock's Legacy adventure arc, they are likely to be drawn to Haarlock's Folly, as it is the temporary precinct of the Adeptus Arbites. Thus, it is an obvious potential source of information and allies.

THE SHADOW OF THE FOLLY

The tower of the Haarlock's Folly casts a long shadow, and not only in the physical universe. Any character within it with the Psyniscience Skill will immediately know when setting foot inside that there is some cold darkness to the place that weighs heavily on a Psyker's mind. Psychic Power used in the Folly have their Thresholds increased by +2, and Telepathy and Divination is almost impossible, revealing only disquieting impressions of icy blackness.

LOCATION DETAILS

Haarlock's Folly has a number of important areas and locations within it that, because of its importance to the events of **DAMNED CITIES** and the likelihood that the Acolytes will return here several times, are separately detailed in the following sections. At any one time, there are around thirty Arbiters and about the same number again in support staff and servitors present in the tower, representing about one-third of the total Adeptus Arbites presence in Sinophia Magna. Any skilled eye realises that this small number is woefully inadequate for a city of this size.

THE EXTERIOR

Haarlock's Folly is a tall, square-sided tower of black stone with a needle-like roof of tarnished bronze that points at the leaden Sinophian sky. Its effect is to exude power overlooking the city as it does. Its form is much at odds with the mute colours and ornamented architecture of the rest of the Sinophia Magna. Beneath its roof are three major levels, each with several distinct compartments and sub-floors. The highest level supports high, arched windows. At its base is a stepped entrance leading to a set of high metal doors. The doors are set beneath an archway carved with images of spiders crawling across a web in which stars are caught. Above this, a large, etched metal plaque bearing the fist-and-wings symbol of the Adeptus Arbites has been recently placed.

Haarlock's Folly sits on a promontory of rock a short distance away from the cliffs overlooking the dark waters of the Saint's Mouth and is ringed by a newly raised wall made up of prefabricated rockcrete slabs topped with armoured walkways, barbed wire, and a gate watchtower mounting a heavy stubber and searchlight covering the approach.

Within the compound wall and off to one side a number of black Rhino APCs and ground cruisers sit under a flak board and tarpaulin hanger awning. The outskirts of the city proper begin a half mile away along the cliff to the west.

THE GROUND FLOOR

Beyond the double metal doors, the entire ground floor is a high-roofed hall. The hall is clad in black and white chequered marble, now plastered partly over by votive parchments, signs bearing morally approved slogans, ordinance papers, and purity seals, punctuated by a series of solid brass doors. The floor is tiled in black and white, scuffed by the tramping of muddy boots. A grating sits in the center of the floor, inlaid in brass, showing the device of a black sun and golden spider.

An armoured Arbiter sits at a brass lectern by the armoured doors and double checks the credentials of any who pass into or out of the building. Behind the lectern is a steel-cased cogitator unit with viewing screen, the power cables of which snake incongruously away over the polished floor. The officer behind the lectern issues a ring of heavy brass keys to authorised visitors; these keys open the locked interior doors and the brass doors in the entrance hall that access the stair wells.

There are three main doors leading off the entrance hall, each guarded by an impassive gun servitor, one in each corner. Each of the three doors is wrought and framed with solid brass several inches thick. Behind each door is an antechamber empty of décor and each with a single caged elevator. Each elevator ascends or descends to a single level of the Folly. From right to left as the visitor enters: The first goes up to the second level, the second goes to the first level and the third goes down to the cellars. Each door and elevator is accessed by a separate key issued by the officer behind the lectern; the key opens the door to the lift beyond and also automatically takes the lift to the appointed level. All the key holes for the doors are the mouths or eyes of individual brass death masks fitted to the walls long ago. Each has a gilded spider branded in the forehead and beneath them reads the same motto: 'The future is ours.'

THE FIRST LEVEL

This floor was originally a series of vaulted chambers and anterooms, possibly a library or museum of objects assembled by the Haarlocks. Long ago emptied of its fixtures and exhibits, now it has been crudely adapted to function as quarters for the small force of Arbitrators and auxiliary staff. Its space has been divided up into small cubicles by sheets of flak board and thick tent canvas. Each cell is a living space with a bunk house for two, a pair of locked steel chests for gear and positions, a single latrine pot with a metal cover, a wash stand, and a devotional icon of the Emperor in judgement over the damned. The room's tall walls are covered with shelves, columned plinths, and the few remaining empty display cases—all shrouded with dusty sheets. Tall windows set into each wall once must have given a superb view in every direction, but these have been sealed over by armoured shutters with slot-like firing loops, letting in a little daylight. The air has a strange smell of the dust overlaid with the raw musk of human living.

Arms Vault

Also on this level, a small windowless side-chamber has been recently fitted with a secure door for use as the Precinct House's small armoury. This door remains locked and guarded by a mono-tasked gun servitor (see page 340 of the DARK

(see page 340 of the DARK HERESY Rulebook)

QUESTIONING THE ARBITRATORS

If given proof of the Acolytes' authority, the Arbiters will answer any questions in a firm, no-nonsense manner. They are a dour bunch, even for Adeptus Arbites. Skilled observation from the Acolytes reveals some to be borderline insubordinate or disenchanted with their posting, whilst others conceal self-control issues, simmering resentments, and other behaviours unbecoming a servant of the God-Emperor's Law. The reason for this hidden antipathy is threefold. First, many of them were not of the highest calibre in the first place, hence their posting here. Second, they are understaffed and badly overworked. Their morale has suffered, and each is regularly committed to double shifts simply guarding Imperial assets and fighting off looters and criminal vermin. The third reason is the psychic contamination of the daemon's wakefulness in the Folly and Skarmen's sorcery, which has begun to cloud their minds and slowly taint their souls.

HERESY Rulebook) at all times. Only Skarmen and the Arbites armourer (an officer called Lana Rubrico, already brought under the Mirror Daemon's influence) have access within.

The armoury contains a number of additional combat shotguns, autoguns, stub automatics, and web guns, plus a handful of more specialised weapons such as grenade launchers, heavy stubbers, disposable missile launchers and long-las rifles. The armoury also contains several thousand rounds of ammunition and a cache of explosives.

THE SECOND LEVEL

The second level contains a number of separate suites of rooms, chambers, and what were clearly once libraries and private quarters. Although much of this level remains disused or sealed off, one former library has being converted into a makeshift control room and is crammed with bulky vox-apparatus and cogitator cells, auto-scribes, pict-viewers and plotters powered by portable generators. A large map of the city is weighed down on a circular stone table at the centre of the room. This control room is manned and guarded at all times, and several servo-skulls hover in its shadowy upper reaches.

Opening off the control room are several private chambers and offices for the senior Adeptus Arbites officers—including Constantine, who has his own set of rooms. Up a brief spiral stair are the offices of Marshal Skarmen, housed in what appears to have been formerly an observatory, judging by the rich web of astronomical and astropathic imagery contained in the murals that cover the walls of the circular chamber. At the centre of the office sits a large, battered steel desk obviously salvaged from elsewhere. Apart from a single chair, a gun rack, and a large Imperial flag placed on the wall, the room is otherwise empty.

The Secret Chamber in the Spire

Behind the flag in Skarmen's office lies a concealed door in the wall. Discovering this requires passing a **Very Difficult (–30) Search Test**. Beyond the door is a long, winding marble staircase leading to a circular tower room—a perfect copy of Skarmen's below. In this room stands two ornate full length mirrors. One mirror is whole and undamaged, in which the Daemon dwells. The other is broken, slowly being re-assembled by Skarmen piece by piece.

THE CELLARS

The Folly's sub-levels are unadorned affairs whose corridors and chambers are covered floor to ceiling in dark, age-pitted metal plates. Lit only by strings of hazard lights the Arbites have installed along the utilised areas, the three main cellar areas have been divided up in order of their descending depth. All levels are accessed through the single cage elevator shaft. Additionally, two ventilation tunnels terminate at ground level at the exterior of the tower, but these are constantly locked and gated at each entry point.

Sub-Cellar 1: Holding Cells & Interrogation Rooms

Several large cellars in this area have been partitioned off using pre-fabricated wire-mesh cages to create makeshift holding cells, and several nearby sealed chambers on this level have been hooked up with pict-systems and recording gear for use as interrogation rooms.

At least one Arbites Custodian (use the Enforcer profile on page 339 of the **DARK HERESY** Rulebook) is on duty in this level at all times, assisted to by two tasked servitor drones equipped with implanted shock mauls who act as gaolers and watchmen (see page 344 of the **DARK HERESY** Rulebook).

Not intended for long-term incarceration, the cells have 1d5 occupants at any one time, each awaiting due processing and judgement for crimes and suspected deviance against Imperial Law.

Sub-Cellar 2: Generatorium and Stores

This lower level is all but dark and deserted, given over to the maintenance of the Folly. It contains a mixture of salvaged and repaired machinery that keeps much of the Folly's amenities and power requirements met. It also houses a servitor repair bay and various dry stores.

Sub-Cellar 3: Cold Store and Mortuary

The deepest level of the Folly is a vast, echoing, cathedral-like space. Its wall is braced with great iron buttresses and ornamented with the shapes of screaming beasts and wrathful angels jutting forth, as if they had somehow been fused alive with the metalwork around them. This huge and sinister chamber is cold enough to make breath frost in the still and silent air, a fact that has been exploited by the Folly's new residents for its use as cold storage and a mortuary.

Set at some distance away from the coffin-like rows of the storage area, a large area perhaps 20 metres square has been partitioned off with metal framework dividers hung with frosty, semi-transparent plasteel sheeting open to the air. This is the mortuary. Inside, a veritable maze of hanging partitions—some marked with arcane bio-hazard symbols—separate a series of meat lockers, examination equipment bays, surgical facilities, and dozens of autopsy gurneys. The mortuary is the domain of the Biologis-Adept Talanis, and he is attended by several servo-skulls and servitors. Talanis has been mentally subjugated by Skarmen and the Mirror Daemon, and his mortuary has served as the source of Skarmen's Risen servants. A detailed account of Talanis's personality and motivations can be found in the Dramatis Personae section on page 27. For Talanis, use the Tech-adept profile on page 345 of the **DARK HERESY** Rulebook.

Sub-Cellar 4: The Catacombs

Unbeknownst to all but Skarmen and his victims, the Folly's mortuary level also provides access to a series of ancient catacombs and tunnels. These passageways extend down into the rock on which the Folly is built. They pass under the causeway and ultimately into the cellars and sewers of the Celestine Warf. These tunnels are nightmarish places: lightless, half-flooded, and choked with the filth and rotting sea detritus of centuries. Here, in the abyssal blackness immediately beneath the Folly, the Risen await their master's command. They use the tunnels to connect to an abandoned warehouse on the edge of the Celestine Warf, where they pick up whatever transport Skarmen has proved for them to go about their bloody work in the city.

At the beginning of the adventure, Skarmen (using lengthy infernal rites given to him by the daemon) has succeeded in creating eight Risen from the bodies of murder victims in the mortuary. One Risen was destroyed in the murder of Bal Grey, and two of the earliest created have begun to mutate. No more than four at once have so far been dispatched to any single murder, but this may change given the increasing difficulty of his intended targets.

See page 64 for profiles for the Risen: powerful, daemon-tainted walking dead.

ENCOUNTER: A LATE BUT WELCOME RECEPTION

Once the Acolytes find their way to the Folly they are met at its gates by an apologetic Arbites officer, Fihad Constantine, who becomes the Acolytes' point of contact with the Imperial authorities on Sinophia (such as they are) and potentially a very valuable ally as matters unfold. A detailed account of Constantine's personality and motivations can be found in the Dramatis Personae section on page 23 and his profile on page 59.

Read aloud or paraphrase the following:

As you pass through the gate, you see a tall figure in a black armoured greatcoat with a low-slung bolter. He has the rank insignia of a junior marshal and moves toward you with purpose. He draws close and introduces himself as Fihad Constantine, Adjutant to the Arbites Proctor Marshal of Sinophia, saying:

"Welcome, honoured servants of the most Holy Ordos, to Sinophia Magna. I can only offer my regrets that I was not able to meet you in person with a delegation at the starport, but miscommunication and an operational emergency here prevented it. The Marshal has appointed me to be your contact here and offer you whatever assistance in this matter I can, my pressing duties permitting. I am honoured to play what part I can in your divinely appointed work to root out heresy and purge the unclean."

Constantine is a slim, vigorous young man with dark eyes and blonde hair. He treats the Acolytes with genuine respect and mention the fortuitousness of their arrival, as only hours previously another murder fitting the pattern was discovered. He has ordered the crime scene preserved and can arrange their transport to the location as soon as they wish.

Constantine's first act is to take them into the Folly and up to his office, where he has plain but likely welcome refreshments brought to them, and if any are injured (possibly due to the attack on the river) he immediately has them treated by an Arbites Medicae (this NPC possesses the Medicae Skill of 40).

What Constantine Knows

Constantine is open to questions and does not conceal any information regarding the matter at hand. He knows the details of the murders as reported—he, after all wrote and submitted the initial report—and can fill them in with details of the latest murder, that of the known criminal Bal Grey.

He can also elaborate from his perspective the rise in tensions between the nobility and the Undertow, as well his personal distaste for the current balance of power on Sinophia, which he mostly doesn't understand but is sworn to respect so long as it doesn't contravene Imperial law.

If pressed on the Acolytes' lack of reception, he apologises again for the breach of protocol. However, he does not toady to them, and if they are particularly abrasive, he lapses into guarded civility. If they wish to meet with Skarmen, he voxes up to his office and arrange it, but won't be argued with about Skarmen's decision not to greet them personally.

What Aid is Offered

Constantine makes no bones that the Arbites on Sinophia are desperately stretched at the moment, and he cannot offer them a standing detachment of men or material, but he can offer the following assistance to their investigations:

- Access to the Arbites Criminal and Suspect records and files.
- The use of the Folly's facilities to sleep, interrogate suspects, or conduct medical examinations in the mortuary.

- He will, if they wish, place an unmarked ground car (and if needs be a driver) at their disposal.
- Replenishment of sundries (such as ammunition, medipacks, and so forth) within reason.
- Offer as much time as he can personally spare to help them if required, as well as his judgement and local knowledge as much as his current duties allow. He cannot be spared to accompany or assist them full–time, however, by Skarmen's direct order.
- Arrange appointments and petition meetings with the Sinophian authorities and noble houses as needed.

He also gives each of them a personal encrypted vox with access to the secured Arbites channels, and an emergency distress code to bring them assistance when needed. He also informs them regrettably that signal strength and vox traffic in Magna is often plagued with interference and deliberate jamming, particularly in the areas known as the Sinks and the Shadow Manses.

OPTIONAL ENCOUNTER: AN INTERVIEW WITH THE MARSHAL

The Acolyte's may demand a meeting with Marshal Skarmen, which is swiftly arranged and takes place in Skarmen's office. Skarmen is respectful but brusque, and iron in his resolve that his Arbiters can offer no further aid unless presented with an immediate threat. If the Acolytes attempt to pull rank, he claims justifiably that to pull Arbitrators off other tasks would be an unforgivable dereliction of duty. If asked for his personal opinions, he offers them. On the matter of the murders, whilst admitting the possibility of a heretical or moral threat,

DISCREPANCIES IN THE OFFICIAL RECORD

Acolytes paying close attention to the minutia of the investigation may (with suitable Intelligence or Security Tests) begin to notice minor but nagging discrepancies with the official investigation records held by the Adeptus Arbites. Certain forensic files will be incomplete or filled with partially corrupted data; the official record may reflect delays in answering alerts from the murder victim's homes, evidence misplaced, and so on. Such faults are quite believable without malign cause, particularly given how hard-pressed the Arbites are, but taken together, they are enough to raise suspicion. This will particularly be the case if the Acolytes compare the official reports with eyewitness testimony, or discover that without the personal diligence of Constantine, who issued the Astropathic alert to the Holy Ordos as regulations dictated given the crimes' nature and potential repercussions, the murders on Sinophia would not have been reported at all…

Skarmen offers his belief that they are likely merely extreme elements of Sinophia Magna's major factions showing the depths to which they will sink. Finally, he voices his concern that the Acolytes, as servants of the Ordos, are better placed to ultimately judge the matter.

A detailed account of Skarmen's personality and motivations can be found in the Dramatis Personae section on page 24 and his profile on page 58.

Note that one option for **DAMNED CITIES** is for Marshal Skarmen to remain distant and mysterious, which helps maintain the noir mood of the adventure. One way to keep this feeling going is to keep the Acolytes from contacting or meeting with Skarmen. They can just miss him at the headquarters, he can be busy in a meeting in some remote location, or they can only get the occasional secondhand message passed on from other Arbitrators. This method can add to the atmosphere of tension and suspicion in this adventure.

OPTIONAL ENCOUNTER: ON THE SLAB

The Acolytes may wish to see the bodies of the victims firsthand, in which case Constantine escorts them down to the bitterly cold mortuary to talk to Biologis-Adept Talanis. The adept emotionlessly details the violence done to the bodies and the superhuman force required to inflict it, but his account is edited to remove any forensic clues as to the true nature of the attackers involved. Whilst he answers questions, Talanis does not volunteer additional information himself.

The remains of Zamura Rolart, Senh-Ar Dole, and Sur'Seculo are all contained in the mortuary. Callisto's body, however, was destroyed before the pattern was identified. See The Shattered Mirror on page 28 and the Player Handout on page 67 for more information on these killings. It is important to note that the corpses were nearly rent limb from limb.

ENCOUNTER: THE CORPSE OF BAL GREY

Bal Grey is the latest victim of the mysterious attackers, slain only hours before the Acolytes' arrival in orbit. Bal Grey was trusted muscle and a reliable fence for the Undertow. He was killed because he had in his possession a fragment of wondrous mirror once recently given him by a slaver and Rag-King called Juvinal Priator (see The Shattered Mirror on page 28). He lived and died in a rundown hab at the edge of the infamous District XIII of Sinophia Magna. See pages 15-16 for more information on this area.

As Bal Grey was murdered only a few hours before the Acolytes arrived in Sinophia Magna, Constantine has ordered the scene to be preserved for them, and the Acolytes may well decide to go and look at the scene of this latest attack and gather information firsthand as one of their first ports of call.

This encounter is intended to be visited early on in the adventure and to act as a means of both setting the scene for players in terms of the nature of the city and its denizens and introducing the involvement of the Undertow. The location as detailed assumes that the Acolytes go to examine the scene using their Inquisitorial authority to move around, question people, and therefore not be shot by the Arbites!

LOCATION DETAILS

The Acolytes arrive in a narrow street in District XIII, which is lined on both sides with moulding garrets. It is close to the river; a light mist is rising, and the air is scented with damp and the smell of stale food. The road is sealed off by an armoured unit of Adeptus Arbites. The body of Bal Grey is in his two-room hab on the fourth floor. Block residents have been ordered to stay in their habs, and little can be heard but the growl of the Arbites Rhino, which has its engine running and its pintle-mounted heavy stubber manned in preparation for trouble.

The fourth floor is splattered with dried blood; there are still chunks of flesh on the floor of the landing, and one of the three doors stands open. The smell is horrific. Inside Grey's hab unit, the corpse is twisted across the centre of the floor. It is clad only in a pair of dirty military fatigue trousers. A discarded pump shotgun with a mangled barrel lies on the floor next to it. The cause of death is clear: The corpse's head and chest have been smashed in and the left arm ripped out of its socket, and the blood pooled on the floor is slowly congealing in a halo around it. A pair of old PDF dog tags confirms the corpse's identity as Bal Grey.

INTERACTIONS AT THE MURDER SCENE

On arrival, the Acolytes and Constantine (if he accompanies them) are greeted with a mixture of impatience and grudging deference. The dozen or so Arbitrators who have been left guarding a corpse in the slums for the last several hours are keen to leave the area and return to base. They offer no help or information that is not asked for, save to say that since their last report, a second, unknown body has been found in a nearby alleyway.

Examining the Scene

The reinforced wooden door of the hab has been broken through with brute force, and the chains and locks have been smashed away from their mountings. There are two rooms within, a bedroom and a tiny bathroom, and the hab unit shows signs of both a struggle and a hasty, crude search by the attackers. There is a mattress on the floor of the bedroom and a promethium burner in the corner. A few books and a copy of the Imperial Infantryman's Uplifting Primer had been stacked neatly on a small set of shelves. Marks from shotgun fire can be seen around the door. From the door to the centre of the room, a dozen empty shell cases litter the floor, and the room still stinks of gunfire.

An old ammunition box lies open on the floor near an open hole in the floor where the boards have been pulled up. The box is filled with soiled and damp cartel bonds and a few Imperial Thrones. A piece of thick red fabric that had been clearly wrapped around something now lies discarded next to the ammo box.

A success on a **Challenging (+0) Search Test** also finds a dozen vials of Ghostfire Pollen Extract (see page 184 of THE INQUISITOR'S HANDBOOK for details) in a hidden recess behind the lavatory.

The Body in the Alleyway

In an alleyway outside the house, a second mutilated body has been found whose condition represents another mystery of its own. Clearly showing the marks of multiple shotgun blasts, it lays untouched and guarded by an Arbitrator. Anyone who stops to examine it notices that the flesh of the corpse is greenish and slightly bloated, as if the corpse had been dead for more than a few hours, and surprisingly little blood is on the body or ground around it.

Anyone who makes a successful **Challenging (+0) Search Test** on the body, despite the gaping chest wounds caused by the shotgun blasts that felled it, finds a series of strange marks cut into the corpse's flesh around the base of its neck, as well as the presence of what appear to be extensive stitched wounds.

Proper medical examination either here or back at the Mortuary reveals a good deal more: A successful **Very Easy (+30) Medicae Test** reveals that the corpse died at least three days ago. The shotgun blasts that felled it were both much more recent and, curiously, post mortem. Two or more Degrees of Success reveals that the arms and hands are covered in bloodless cuts and splintered wood.

A Feeling of Being Watched

Once the Acolytes have been in the hab for five or more minutes (or if the GM feels that the investigation is winding down), they should take a **Challenging (+0) Perception Test**. This is a visual test, and any Acolytes who succeed spot a dark figure on the rooftop opposite. Two or more degrees of success means that the Acolyte notices the dark, broad-brimmed rain hat and long coat. If the Acolytes are obvious in their discovery, the figure flees, possibly resulting in a foot chase through the alleyways or rooftops. The figure is a trusted member of the Mandato division of the Enforcers sent by Enforcer General Khan to find out what is going on (use the Skulker profile on page 344 of the DARK HERESY rulebook if a combat ensues for this individual) and will die rather than face capture. If the GM is planning to employ Spectre Cell 17 at a later point, this watcher himself is being watched and may well be later discovered dead by any Acolytes who catch onto his trail.

If the man is captured by the Acolytes, he is tight-lipped and uncooperative. He carries upon him a tracking signal that alerts Enforcer General Khan that his agent has been captured, and Khan quickly steps in to have the man released.

OTHER LINES OF INQUIRY

The recent murder of Bal Grey and the other leads and clues that spin off it are fully detailed in the following section. However, a number of other possible avenues and tangents exist for the Acolytes to follow. Rather than simply 'railroad' them down this line, the GM should to let them follow their leads until they naturally play out, or give up such information in a logical manner. These might include:

Off-World Cults, New Arrivals to Sinophia, and the Trail of Money: A convenient location to gather this info is the Turning Hand (see the Sinophia Gazetteer on page 17). The Turning Hand is also an excellent place to gather rumours from unbiased outsiders about the spiteful intrigues and factionalism of the Sinophians themselves. It also rents out secure rooms if lodging at Haarlock's Folly holds no appeal (which is quite likely, particularly if there is a Psyker in the Acolyte team), and is also a good place to hire extra muscle and make arms deals at decent rates.

The Nobility: Directly approaching Sinophia's nobility is unlikely to be helpful, as they have too many simmering resentments and too much to hide to make small talk with agents of the Throne. Persistence, however, will get the Acolytes an interview with Margrave Cal Sur'Maywroth (see the Dramatis Personae on page 25) whose primary interests will be in blaming the Undertow and the incompetency of the Adeptus Arbites. He may well try to bribe or manipulate the Acolytes into killing off the Undertow Rag Court, or perhaps praise them for protecting one of his barges from attack (see Dead in the Water on page 35).

The Haarlock Connection, the Strange Phenomena at the Folly, Myths and Legends of Sinophia: The Arbites themselves are entirely ignorant of this, whilst the Sinophians themselves have an almost maniacal talent for self-deception and selective memory when it comes to their world's past. Inquiries might lead the Acolytes to the Tarot Tellers at the Turning Hand. The Tarot Tellers presage disaster, and spin cryptic portents about a broken tower, a traitor king and prisoners freed. Any efforts to enlist the aid of the blessed Ministorum find the cathedral in District I (see the Sinophian Gazetteer on page 13) dominated by the worst sort of worldly, venial and insular priests—sure to enrage any pious cleric among the Acolytes' ranks. Persistent and clever inquiry, however, leads the Acolytes to the chambers of Eupheme Tassel (see Dramatis Personae on page 25 and Unvarnished Truth on page 50). This young woman knows a great deal about Sinophia's real history, and is not afraid to speak of it if correctly approached.

Talking to the Residents

The following information can be gleaned from the locals with sufficient persuasion:

The Story of Bal Grey

Taking time to question the residents of the block and street reveals that Bal Grey was part of the Undertow, a junior boss or Rag-Baron. However, most people liked him more than others of his ilk—he was no rabid beast or random killer, and only took on those who crossed him or his employers. It was known he was an ex-PDF sergeant and ran his own crew (who have subsequently faded away), primarily providing muscle for hire and making sure trouble stayed away from the area.

The Assailants

Four figures in cloaks and hoods were seen in the street going up the stairs shortly before the sounds of violence and gunshots started. Afterward, the four men came out again, as calm as you please, and one staggered off round the side of the building—but the others paid him no mind and disappeared into the rain just afterward.

Additional Information

Three or more Degrees of Success on an Inquiry Test results in an old man in the hab underneath Grey's talking about someone called Juvinal Priator who:

"Was another of them you know? A Rag-King and a bad one; a buyer and seller of meat if you catch my drift. There was bad blood between them there, but they did some deal and Bal got paid off with something flat all wrapped up in red cloth. Used to be some real tension between the two of them; a few of Bal's lads cut up one of Priator's, and Priator's skinners gave one of his Bal's best girls to the Saint—but all that was sorted out, best of friends now, everyone was talking about it."

OPTIONAL ENCOUNTER: INVESTIGATING THE SINKS

The Sinks are the slum district near the river (Drusus's Flow), the sea, and the swamps of the margins. Districts V, X, and particularly XIII are especially notorious as the rotting warrens in which the desperate and forgotten eke out an existence. These are areas dominated by the organised criminality of the Undertow and filled with a brooding resentment and fear of the violence that those who live close to the street can feel coming. Since the killing of Bal Grey and other members of Sinophia Magna's criminal underclass took place in the slum areas, it is possible that the Acolytes might wish to chase down leads in the Sinks; information about the Undertow, details about the previous murder victims, or the scenes of murders which have already occurred are all things that might draw Acolytes into the slums. This location represents not a single building or encounter within the Sinks, but the general character and nature that can be experienced by Acolytes who go looking for answers amongst the dregs of Sinophia's forgotten humanity.

LOCATION DETAILS

The local atmosphere is hostile, with people staring from behind half-closed doors and groups of figures in damp cloaks and hoods on corners. It is raining, and the river carries the strong smell of mould. The buildings are plastered and in poor repair with broken windows and mould-scabbed walls. Most windows are covered with rotting wooden shutters, and doorways are closed with warped wooden doors or rusted metal gates. Many buildings are deserted and falling into ruin; their tiled roofs collapsing, the plastered walls crumbling in on themselves. The cellar of any building is filled with at least a foot of stinking water, and everywhere are the vermin skittering or skulking out of sight. Within any building inhabited by people is a pungent smell of sweat and human waste, mingling with the smell of boiling vegetable matter. Most inhabited buildings have few residents, and most rooms are filled with rubbish and detritus.

Getting Around in the Sinks

Even if the Acolytes have an address or a general location of somewhere they are looking for, it is not easy to keep one's bearings within the slum districts of the Sinks. The GM should impose Skill Tests appropriate to the approach being taken by the Acolytes—unless they've managed to find themselves a reliable guide. Arbites-provided maps won't be that much help either in this maze of blind alleys, canals, collapsed buildings, transient shanks, and shanties.

Appropriate Skill Tests would be Navigation Tests (if the Acolytes are using a map or directions) or Charm Tests (if they are finding their way by asking the inhabitants). Degrees of Success should make their search easier and faster; Degrees of Failure makes their search longer and more difficult. The finding of a location should be treated as a prime opportunity to let the Acolytes have an interesting encounter.

Note that the Sinks makes a great place for the Acolytes to discover some of the rumours from the sidebar on this page.

Making Friends and Influencing People

If the Acolytes wish to find a particular person, or get their questions answered whilst in the slum districts, they have to work against the natural resentment and suspicion of the residents. As a guideline, all Interaction Skill Tests used to gather information about people should be Challenging (+0) if the Acolytes act as agents of authority and lean on their Inquisitorial credentials. Positive modifiers may be given if the Acolytes disguise their official nature effectively and spread a few thrones around.

The most effective way of getting information is with bribery, either with money or goods, and the GM should assign positive modifiers to Tests to gather information when such methods are used. Other methods of eliciting the required information, such as intimidation, may prove more effective. Creativity should be rewarded with positive modifiers to Intimidation Skill Tests. This more aggressive approach brings a full-scale Undertow crew in to confront the Acolytes more quickly and with greater numbers (see Circling Wolves further on in this section).

Making Contact with the Undertow Directly

The Undertow is everywhere in the Sinks, and every man, woman, and child is involved with the group in some way. It may well be that the Acolytes meet the lower, more brutish, ranks of the Undertow whether they wish to or not (see Circling Wolves in the next section). If, however, they wish to make contact with more senior members of the criminal organisation, they may do so via almost any resident of the slum districts (everyone knows someone who knows someone in the slums) but are treated with great suspicion. Bribes and good use of Skills such as Charm and Deceive get them an early meeting with senior members of the Undertow if they dare go (see The Rag Court on page 45).

Circling Wolves

If the Acolytes ask questions about the previous murder victims and their relationship to the Undertow, they attract the attention of the Undertow thugs who lurk in every rotten crevice of the slum districts. The Undertow believe they are under attack and assume that strangers asking questions (especially if they look official) are a threat to be removed.

A short time after the Acolytes have taken such actions, all should make **Challenging (+0) Awareness Skill Tests**. Those who pass realise that they are being shadowed by hooded figures. The thugs intend to eventually box in the Acolytes and attack to kill. There should be approximately twice as many Undertow thugs as there are Acolytes to fight them off, divided roughly so that they attack from at least two directions at once. If the Acolytes have road transport, the thugs start by ramming it off the road with a cargo hauler or otherwise disabling it. Use the profile for Undertow Muscle (see pages 65-66 in Appendix I: NPCs and Antagonists) to represent them.

The number of assailants should be doubled if the Acolytes used excessive violence and intimidation to get information off the locals. If any of the Undertow thugs are captured, they break after only moderate interrogation. They reveal that the Enforcers are trying to muscle in on their turf and take over their rackets, and that a number of their bosses have been killed. They also state that they assumed the Acolytes were working for Enforcer General Xiabius Khan as off-world freelancers.

Rumours

- "The Enforcers did it! They killed the Judiciary. He refused to pay them and they killed him. Now Khan is in charge, and there'll be blood in the streets."
- "The Quorum has been infiltrated by the Malfians with over half the council in the pay of off-worlders. The rest is just a cover-up to mask their takeover."
- "The Rag-Kings have made a deal with the wreckers from the stone lands for reinforcements. They are arming the cannibals and have promised the Quorum will be filled with the gnawed bones of its former masters before long!"
- "They're rounding up prisoners and massacring them out at the old abandoned arena on the stonelands arteria; some say hundreds were gunned down just to slake the Enforcers' bloodlust."
- "A skimmer carriage belonging to old Lord Gualoa was knocked out of the air with a missile over the Prime. It crashed into the Cathedral, I heard."
- "The Enforcer General has unleashed caged witches from beneath the Sanctum; they are going to rip the souls from the Judiciary's killers to question them and will do the same to anyone else who gets in their way."
- "The Empty Men have returned! We're all going to die, I tell you!"

THE FRIENDS OF BAL GREY

If the Acolytes are successful in their investigations around the death of Bal Grey, the GM should feel free to add in extra clues and sources of information as is warranted, particularly if the Acolytes successfully hunt down some of Grey's former crew in the Sinks. They know nothing of the death itself, but espouse the theory that its some sort of revenge attack by the nobility, or the beginning of the Sanctum Enforcers muscling in on the Undertow's territory. If the unnatural nature of the crimes is pointed out to them, wild theories such as "the Nobles are all in league with dark witches" or "it must be renegade xenos" begin to fly from their lips.

There are, however, two very solid leads that can come out investigations into the Sinks and Magna's underbelly: the Undertow connection and Grey's past associates.

Grey recently was paid off by another Rag-King, Juvinal Priator, who is rumoured also to now be dead or gone underground. (This leads to The Late Juvinal Priator.)

Grey's killing is very similar to an attack on a chop-shop called the Worm's End (a slum canteen) several nights ago, an incident that the Arbites are not aware of, at least officially. (This leads to On the Run.)

OPTIONAL ENCOUNTER: THE LATE JUVINAL PRIATOR

Should the Acolytes learn the name of Bal Grey's former rival and sometime business partner, Juvinal Priator, they might naturally wish to track him down. He is a somewhat infamous figure with a reputation as a slaver, killer, and warp dabbler known to both the Enforcers and the Adeptus Arbites.

Inquiries in the Sinks that succeed through violence, intimidation, or bribery (see Optional Encounter: Investigating the Sinks on page 42 for guidance on handling these interactions) reveal the popular rumour that he is dead or gone to ground. The location of his most likely hideout, a nameless, disused fish-gutting plant on the Celestine Wharf (see pages 17-18), is known to many in the Sinks. The Sanctum Enforcers have records of this hideout, but the Adeptus Arbites do not.

PRIATOR'S HIDEOUT

The shuttered plant is a sprawling, wreckage-strewn mess, rusted and reeking of rotted fish and industrial effluent. Security is light, consisting of a few chained wire-mesh fences and crudely barricaded doors, although a careful search of the exterior also reveals a heretek-made cyber-mastiff with its back snapped, partly submerged in a silt-filled sinkhole.

Inside the main building is a maze of broken machinery and trash, gantry-ways and hoists, lit only by the weak light and rain coming in from the roof. At the centre of the building is what was formerly the dwelling place and work quarters of Priator's slaver crew. This area, based around a now-cold drum fire, is strewn with old mattresses, drug paraphernalia, worthless trinkets, mismatched and damaged furniture, spoiled food, empty bottles, vandalised statues, and other random junk. Three twisted corpses lie around the fire drum, all having died some days ago by their level of putrefaction. Around them are broken blades and spent shell casings—but no guns. One corpse, despite its condition, was clearly singled out for worse treatment than the others, each limb having been snapped at distorted angles. Looped silver chains around this corpse's neck are heavy with fingerbones, runic talismans, and other signs of petty warpcraft.

Nearby, two large slurry tanks have been converted to slave cages by the addition of crude wire mesh panels and chained manacles. The cages are open and empty but show signs of recent occupancy. Opposite from them, hidden by a hanging tarpaulin, is Priator's private domain, now ransacked but strewn with scribbled notes, damaged data-slates, a shattered oil lamp, and scattered collections of crude fetishes, knives, and branding irons.

AMBUSH

Whilst the wider authorities are unaware of Praitor's death, the Undertow most assuredly is not. The Rag Queen Hesul has set a watch on the dead man's hideout to see who might arrive in search of Priator or perhaps return to the scene of the crime. This ambush party tries to close in stealthily once the Acolytes reach the inner hideout.

The ambush party consists of one Skulker (see page 344 of the **DARK HERESY** Rulebook) named Georg Lussk and a number of Undertow Muscle (see pages 65-66 in Appendix I: NPCs and Antagonists) equal to the number of Acolytes in the party.

The ambush raiders are familiar with the plant's layout and so get a +10 bonus in their attempts to sneak up and surround the Acolytes.

Lussk's goal is to take the Acolytes (preferably unarmed, but armed at a push) to see Hesul and the Rag Court, and will do so by force if he find he has no alternative. He begins by demanding surrender rather than attacking on sight. If pressed, he has his men fight to the death whilst he tries to flee. If captured, he readily breaks with little coercion, hoping to achieve by manipulation what he could not by force or persuasion.

Note: This encounter with Lussk can be a bit too direct and threatening for some Acolytes (who may be rightly suspicious and paranoid!). The meeting with the Rag Court is an important moment in this adventure, so the GM may wish to have Lussk approach the Acolytes openly and simply invite them to the meeting (although, his thugs may still remain obvious in the background!).

ENCOUNTER: THE RAG COURT

There are several ways in which the Acolytes might enter a meeting with the governing Rag Court of the Undertow, Sinophia Magna's most powerful crime lords. This may be either through the Acolytes' own design, at the Undertow's invitation once aware of their investigation, or because of the ambush at Priator's hideout.

The Rag Court only agrees to the meeting because it sees advantage in knowing what the Acolytes know, and its members have their own agendas and perspectives on the ongoing crisis. (For detailed accounts of the three crime boss's personalities see the Dramatis Personae on page 26, whilst their profiles may be found in the NPCs and Antagonists appendix on pages 59-60). This encounter is a good opportunity for the GM to keep the investigation on track. For instance, if the Acolytes are still unaware that the connections between the murders are the mirror fragments, Scorn can illustrate this detail for them.

The meeting itself either takes place at a chosen location such an Undertow-owned venue, an abandoned manse, or even private rooms at the Turning Hand (see the Sinophia Gazetteer on page 17). But regardless, the Rag Court does not allow itself to become vulnerable, and each member hase protection nearby and escape routes planned out in advance should things go awry.

Each of the Rag Court has his or her own questions for the Acolytes as to what is happening, but can also provide answers. These can include:

- **[Tiber]** *"The Undertow is not responsible for the murders, but if the Enforcers want a war, they can have a war."*
- **[Hersul]** *"The Judiciary is a weak fool who does what Khan tells him."*
- **[Scorn]** *"The witnesses said the attackers were four men, heavy built and shrouded in rain cloaks."*
- **[Tiber]** *"There was another similar attack, one the Arbiters don't seem to know about, at a run-down chop shop called Worm's End: same pattern, several dead. It might be worth looking into."* (See On the Run on page 46)
- **[Scorn]** (If Spectre Cell 17 is being used) *"We aren't the only ones following you, you know. There are others: Khan's Mandato skulkers now and then, and someone else, we don't know who, off-worlders we think, and they are very, very good at not being seen."*

PORTRAYING THE RAG COURT

The members of the Rag Court each have their own way of dealing with the Acolytes. The following notes help the GM set the scene.

Hesul asks the most questions, but holds back her own opinions. Hesul is the one who informs the Acolytes about Spectre Cell 17. She is scornful of the Acolytes, and is obviously not willing to be friendly.

Tiber asks very few direct questions, but he is quick to offer opinions (and threats!). He is the main source of rumours and speculation, and he is the most eager to go on the offensive to resolve the problem. Tiber treats the Acolytes with the same rough manner he uses on everyone else.

Scorn stays mostly quiet, but he makes it clear that he does not wish to talk to the nobles. He tells the Acolytes about the attack on Worm's End, although he does not know about the fate of Yantra.

THE MATTER OF THE MIRROR

Although they had not made the connection themselves, the Rag Court between them can make several concrete assertions about the mirror fragments if the Acolytes raise the matter. You may use some, or all of these statements:

- **[Tiber]** "Callisto, he was my old boss, he had a 'truth glass' he claimed. I saw it, pretty thing, but I thought it was just a lie to frighten the dregs and the other witless filth."
- **[Hesul]** "Praitor was a petty warp dabbler and would-be daemon bait, not much use at it though. I'd have gutted him for it if he had been. But he collected all sorts of odds and ends, most of it junk. The fool was no true sorcerer, but I wouldn't have put him past running afoul of the real thing sooner or later."
- **[Scorn]** "Throne shine on me. That off-worlder money broker, that perfumed high and mighty Sen-har Dole, he had taken it. What was it he called it? A 'witch-mirror' from some bankrupt noble as collateral for a debt. He tried to sell it to me once, but I have no use for such things. Ha! If I had bought it, why it might be me now lying on the cold slab!"

Scorn also knows the story of the looting of Haarlock's Folly and is clever enough to make the connection having had the tale passed down from his predecessors in the Undertow. He also knows that two of the shards were given to the Judiciary as a payment by the original thieves and said to have been fashioned into hand mirrors so the Judiciary could 'look upon what Haarlock had prized.'

Despite the evidence and connection the mirror fragments and Haarlock's Folly, the Rag Court cannot simply call off hostilities even if they can be convinced that others are to blame. If the meeting ends amicably, they give the Acolytes free passage through their domains—which, whilst not an iron-clad guarantee of safety, is better than nothing. This dubious blessing also adds +10 to any Inquiry Tests made with the Undertow's wider membership.

If the meeting goes particularly well, the Undertow Rag Court also leave an open avenue of communication to the Acolytes and may provide assistance if called on in the adventure's final stages.

OPTIONAL ENCOUNTER: ON THE RUN

Five days before the Acolytes arrival on Sinophia, the Worm's End, a run-down slum canteen, was attacked by Skarmen's Risen to take a fragment of the mirror from an insane dreg known in the slums as Sokken. (See The Shattered Mirror on page 28.) The attack was swift and brutal, and the Worm's End stands broken and gore-splattered to this day. Sokken was killed in the attack, along with several other patrons, the cook, and his son. The authorities were never notified of the assault, but one of the patrons—a down-at-the-heels hab-worker named Lynan Yantra, escaped the slaughter he witnessed. Whilst the attack wasn't reported to the authorities, it has since become the source of rumour in District 13—and those whispers have reached the ears of the Rag-King Scorn.

Yantra himself is still in hiding, moving from one abandoned building to another in the area, and is currently sheltering under the stairwell of a nearby hab-stack. Too afraid to go home or to flee into the city, he's been living like a scavenger, begging for scraps from passersby, but hasn't been able to keep his mouth shut about his fears and is quite easy to find (a **Routine (+10) Inquiry Test**) once the Acolytes know to look for him. A detailed description of Yantra's character can be found on in the Dramatis Personae on page 27.

Note: Another option for this encounter is to have Yantra approach the Acolytes on his own. This method means that many Acolytes will be sympathetic to his cause and more willing to help him.

YANTRA'S TESTIMONY

Should the Acolytes get Yantra to tell them what he knows, he gladly tells them—just not very coherently.

Read aloud or paraphrase the following statements:

"It was old Sokken they came for! I used to see him sometimes down by the wharf, shouting that he was 'returning from the dark cold' and 'the sun will burn black' and such nonsense. He was mad you see, mad or that's what I always thought. Not so sure now, no, no…"

"There was three of them; they just piled into the Worm, one from each side, just killing people! Snapping and mangling them in their bare hands, tearing them to bits! But it was old Sokken they were after, his name they called in those awful dry voices, but he wouldn't give it to them, no he wouldn't. No, he wouldn't give that wrapped-up thing of his willingly, even when they crushed his hands bloody for him to let go!"

"I ducked under the table, saw it all, crawled off before they could catch me and hid, been hiding since. You'll help me won't you? They weren't natural, not at all, I saw one of their faces, there was a hole in his head you see, gunshot, not then but before. You understand you were all dead, they were already dead!"

Yantra's subsequent fate is left up to the Acolytes. If they leave him to his own devices, word may get out (depending on the Acolytes' actions) that the Inquisition is involved. This may prompt Skarmen to accelerate his production of Risen, and it can make things more difficult when dealing with Khan's Enforcers. Alternatively, Yantra is no fool, and if the Acolytes' tell him to keep his mouth shut, he complies.

TRIGGER ENCOUNTER: DEATH IN THE CLOCKWORK COURT

Should the Acolytes' investigations begin to bear fruit, particularly if they show inklings toward researching the Haarlock legend on Sinophia or let it be known they believe a third, unknown faction is involved in the murders, then Skarmen is forced into carrying out a more daring strategy—striking at the heart of the Sinophian Court—to claim two of the remaining fragments of the mirror.

The Clockwork Court and its curious history, as well as the Quorum and the office of the Judiciary, are described in detail in the Sinophian Gazetteer on page 16.

THE INVITATION

This encounter can be triggered in a number of ways.

Firstly, the Acolytes themselves may seek an audience with the Judiciary or the Quorum, particularly if they have learned that he has a fragment of the mirror. Such meetings must be arranged beforehand through proper channels, granting Skarmen his opportunity. Constantine may suggest that Marshal Skarmen can contact the Quorum's factotum and arrange the meeting. Another option is for the Acolytes to display their Inquisitional authority and demand such a meeting.

Alternately, Skarmen (via selective leaking of information) sees to it that the Acolytes' presence is demanded by the Quorum, who wish a private report on their findings into the killing so far. Skarmen also manipulates matters so that the loudest voice in this is Margrave Cal Sur'Maywroth (see the Dramatis Personae on page 25), trusting that subsequent events cast suspicion on a man who, although unconnected to the conspiracy, has much of his own to hide.

Such a request from the ruling planetary authorities (issued via the Adeptus Arbites to the Acolytes) might be delayed, but cannot be legitimately ignored. In this case, the request is authored and signed by Cal Sur'Maywroth and delivered by Marshal Skarmen, who brings it to them and explains he will meet with the Acolytes at the entrance to the Clockwork Court the following day.

Skarmen's Plan

Skarmen's plan is to sneak a number of the Risen past the Court security by having them masquerade as the Inquisitorial Acolytes, knowing that as such they are not be searched or barred access until the very gates of the Quorum. Then, once they are stopped, he will have them wreak as much havoc as possible. Meanwhile Skarmen, using his skills and sorcery, will murder the Judiciary and takes his fragment of the mirror, and another of his Risen will be sent to the chambers of the Keeper of the Rolls for her grandfather's fragment.

Imposters!

When the Acolytes arrive to answer the summons, they are met at the outer halls of the Clockwork Court and delayed by the guards, who display some private confusion about their appearance. Minutes later, Marshal Skarmen walks out from within, arguing loudly with an elderly and hawkish court official.

Skarmen points at the Acolytes and shouts: *"You doddering idiot, they are the honoured agents of the Throne I have come here to meet!"*

The usher gasps. *"The Founder save us, who then have I let into the Court?"*

Then, all hell breaks loose.

Bloody Murder in the Quorum

Lights flicker, die, and then pulse back on at half strength as explosions rumble throughout the building and smoke billows out of the passageway to the inner Court. The Sanctum guards panic and generally get in the way. Skarmen shouts, "With me! Protect the Judiciary!" and disappears into the smoke.

How the Acolytes handle what follows is up to them. Within the Clockwork Court, three of the Risen are playing havoc, killing at random and hurling grenades in an effort to cause as much carnage and confusion as possible. Meanwhile, thanks to sabotage devices planted in the Court's power relays and the psychic static produced by the Risen, the mechanical Clockwork servants have gone haywire. No help is coming for the short term, and all communications and scanner systems have been cut off.

This part of the adventure is a chance for combat- and command-oriented Acolytes to shine in defeating the Risen, as they are the only ones in the vicinity who are able to stop them from conducting a general massacre. This task is made considerably easier if they manage to rally the panicked enforcers into a cohesive fighting force. Towards the end of the battle, Skarmen reappears, smoking bolt pistol in his hand, bruised and bloody from a wound to the head, claiming to have "Killed one of the damned things" in a side corridor, and there is the evidence of a burning corpse to back this up. As soon as the fighting stops, he departs hurriedly after he has made his role in the battle publicly known.

If the Acolytes manage to avert great loss of life, they have earned some measure of respect and gratitude from both the Sanctum Enforcers and the Quorum, a factor that may weigh

well in their favour later in the adventure.

They cannot, however, stop the murder of the Judiciary and his private entourage during the confusion—and the theft of the mirror fragment. Their bodies are found in a private chamber nearby, each killed with a single las-round to the head without a single shot being fired in return—facts from which the Acolytes can deduce what they will.

Note: If the GM has taken the option where Marshal Skarmen is remote and aloof (see page 40), this encounter provides a great opportunity to introduce him to the Acolytes. If this dramatic moment is their first meeting with the Marshal, he may end up impressing them with his aplomb and obvious martial prowess.

THE RISEN

With the risk of exposure high, Skarmen and the daemon have taken extra measures to make sure the Risen are not discovered for what they truly are on their suicide mission. TheRisen are heavy swathed in black bandages and dark green rain cloaks, hidden beneath a psychic illusion that makes them look like Inquisitorial Acolytes from more than half a metre away; a closer look disturbs the psychic veil, allowing the viewer to glimpse the true features of the Risen as if through a heat haze. The number of Risen in this encounter is three, but the GM should adjust this number based on the number of Acolytes, their Rank, and their equipment. For the purposes of this adventure, one Risen for every two or three Rank 4 Acolytes should suffice.

Skarmen has also equipped these Risen with hand cannons (see page 130 of the **DARK HERESY** Rulebook) and two frag grenades (see page 131 of the **DARK HERESY** Rulebook) each, although they quickly lose patience with such toys once the killing begins. Each also carries an incendiary device strapped to his side, which they use to immolate themselves (use the profile for a single Firebomb blast from page 131 of the **DARK HERESY** Rulebook) should they become too damaged to carry on their murderous work.

If asked about the Risen destroyed by Skarmen, he explains that the "creature activated some kind of incendiary device." The panicked crowds nearby do not leave much time for questions in any case.

PART II: BLIND ENEMIES

From this point on, the adventure enters its later stages, and the Acolytes—if they do not act by their own volition—are swept up in the deadly events that rapidly follow in sequence around them. The Acolytes may well have their own ideas of what's really going on and their own suspicions to pursue, but time is now against them and worse is yet to come.

STATE OF TURMOIL— BOILING POINT

The attack on the Clockwork Court has caused a brutal clampdown by the Enforcers, and a wave of vigilantism, reprisals, panic, and looting that has risen in response. The smoke of burnt-out Undertow hideouts drifts past Enforcer roadblocks, and the entire city is reaching a boiling point of violence that may consume it utterly.

The attack on the Judiciary and Clockwork Court has pushed the tense standoff between the Enforcers and Undertow into the beginnings of open warfare. The Enforcers are convinced that the Undertow has the means and will to make a serious attempt to take over control of the city. The Undertow, in turn, are largely convinced that the attack on the Clockwork Court has been mounted by Enforcer General Khan to clear his way to dominating the city, whilst at the same time giving him the perfect pretext to wage open war on the streets of Sinophia Magna.

GAME EFFECTS

With violence, random arrests, and beatings on the streets and bloody reprisal attacks from the Undertow growing ever bolder, people are on edge and likely to react like cornered animals, with nobility shutting themselves up in their manses and the Undertow arming for war.

All investigation and interaction Tests made by the Acolytes should have a positive modifier of no greater than Ordinary (+10). All open efforts at investigation in the locked-down areas bring the attention of the Enforcers, who may be too trigger happy to care about the niceties of Inquisitorial or Arbites authority. Failed Intimidation Tests automatically elicit a violent reaction in those the Acolytes are trying to intimidate, whilst the Undertow are just as likely to shoot first and ask questions later.

SIGHTS AND SOUNDS

The air is tinged with the smell of smoke and burning fuel, and gunfire can occasionally be heard through the blare of sirens. Buildings burn here and there across the city, and roads are blocked by wrecked vehicles in places. The thick smoke drifts across the rooftops. A curfew has been imposed in Prime and the Commercia, and in the nearly deserted streets, black-clad Enforcers can be seen bundling figures into cargo haulers. The Celestine Wharf is alive with activity, with weapons caches being broken open and distributed to the Undertow forces digging into the Sinks.

ENCOUNTER: BEFORE THE STORM

The Acolytes may wish to return to Haarlock's Folly at this point to re-group and re-arm themselves, as well as get an overview of what is going on in the city. They might also be recalled there for debriefing following the attack at the Clockwork Court. The news is not good. The atmosphere at the Folly is even more bleak and oppressive than previously, and only a skeleton crew of Arbites remain at the building, the rest deployed to various sites around the city to guard Imperial facilities such as the Cathedral from a rising tide of disorder, looting, and violence.

Constantine, if absent, re-appears battered and wounded from a gunfight on the Wharf and speaks of bloody Enforcer crackdowns and equally murderous Undertow reprisals all across the city. Skarmen, if encountered, seems on the edge, pacing and restless but strangely triumphant.

If, at this stage, the Acolytes have their own suspicions about Skarmen, they need evidence to make them stick. Simply attacking him in the Folly is likely to prove suicidal without outside help, as they face not only Skarmen and the still loyal Arbites, but also the Mirror Daemon and the Risen (see the NPCs and Antagonists section on page 58). If Skarmen suspects they know of the fragments' importance, or suspect him or some connection to the Folly, he makes sure to keep them busy and away from the Folly as much as he can with false reports and genuine crises until the time is right.

OPTIONAL ENCOUNTER: THE ENFORCER GENERAL

Depending on how things have transpired up to this point, the Acolytes are likely to be summoned before the Enforcer General to explain what they believe is occurring and their actions during the attack on the Clockwork Court. This meeting takes place at the very centre of the Sanctum in the headquarters of the feared Mandato, and how matters progress between the volatile and psychopathic Enforcer General should very much depend on what has gone before.

If the Acolytes have cultivated a relationship that favours the Enforcers or the nobility, or did well in the attack at the court, then Khan is likely to be better disposed toward them. In this case, he warns them that the city is going to descend into a war he intends to start, fight, and win on his own terms rather than wait for the next treacherous blow to land. As for the Acolytes, they can either be part of his plans or stay out of the way….

If the Acolytes have clashed directly with the Enforcers before this, (including unknowingly killing any of their tailing agents), or if they are known to Khan to have had peaceful negotiations with the Undertow bosses, the interview consists of hard questions, veiled threats, and Khan sizing them up personally. If the Enforcer General ends this interview believing that the Acolytes pose a threat to his plans, he marks them for death. Although far too sensible to kill agents of the Inquisition on his own turf, he spares the time to send his disposable and untraceable agents after them in the shape of plainclothes Mandato kill squads at the first opportunity.

The Acolytes may also notice that one of Khan's medals contains a brightly reflective shard of curious glass at its centre; what they do with this knowledge at this stage is up to them.

OPTIONAL ENCOUNTER: UNVARNISHED TRUTH

The following optional encounter is something of a information dump, and based on what has gone before in the game, it can either confirm that the Acolytes are on the right track nudge them in the direction of what's really going on.

Eupheme Tassel sends the Acolytes a message saying that she has discovered something of vital interest to their investigations and she believes that her life is in danger.

Alternately, Eupheme herself could report the ransacking of her chambers during the attack on the Court to the Acolytes, having learned of their interest and presence in the city.

Questioning Eupheme in general potentially reveals much as she knows: the common legend of the thirteen pieces of shattered mirror taken in the looting of Haarlock's Tower, the reputed powers of its fragments, and the infamous history of Erasmus Haarlock himself the tower's last occupant (see The Haarlock Legacy Campaign page 70 for suitable details to furnish the player's with). However, Eupheme has made a dangerous discovery in the aftermath of the attack on the Judiciary.

EUPHEME'S REVELATION

Subsequent to the attack on the Judiciary (including the theft of his mirror) and an attack on her own chambers, Eupheme made a connection that previously had escaped her. She has since researched and translated secret papers belonging to her grandfather, who himself had obtained a mirror fragment and used it for scrying and seeing glimpses of the ancient past and distant worlds reflected in its surface. As his mastery of the fragment increased, he came to understand that the mirror fragments were cursed and held in them daemonic forces that Haarlock alone could control. Her grandfather believed that the fragments were part of a pair of identical mirrors fashioned to bind and control a summoned entity of the warp between them, and that daemon was imprisoned there still, whispering to him in his dreams so long as he used the mirror. Fearing for his sanity and soul, he put aside his shard and sealed it within a laquerwood box guarded with secret wards. He did not touch it again once he suspected its true nature.

His papers also indicated Eupheme's grandfather knew of the locations of three other fragments, including two incorporated into paired gilded hand mirrors in possession of the Judiciary's office. One of these mirrors is still kept as part of the accoutrements of state, and the other was given to Lady Amorite by one of the previous Judiciaries some fifty years ago. The third fragment he saw once at a private ball given by the now-murdered Viscount Hiram Sur'Seculo and recognised it for what it was immediately.

EUPHEME'S MIRROR

The GM has two options about what to do in relation to the disposition of Eupheme's mirror and should choose the one best suited to the way the adventure is playing out.

Option 1—The Mirror is Stolen: The Keeper's chambers were ransacked whilst she was absent during the attack on the Judiciary, and the box that held her grandfather's mirror was broken, its contents missing. In this case it is already in Skarmen's hands.

Option 2—The Mirror is Safe: Eupheme found the box safe with a scorched handprint still smoking on its surface, the wards her grandfather put in place clearly strong enough to keep whatever wished to take it at bay. Eupheme gladly gives the box and the mirror to the Acolytes, freeing herself of danger and passing it on to them…

OPTIONAL ENCOUNTER: THE HOUSE OF AMORITE

The House of Amorite is an ancient pile filled with cobwebs and spoiled grandeur surrounded by an overgrown garden of weeds. Within this once beautiful manse dwells Lady Amorite, consumed by bitterness and loss and clad in rotting finery. She shambles through candlelit rooms from which she has shut out all daylight, rooms filled with things of great worth and beauty that are slowly turning to dust. Waited on by failing servitors, she hates everything and values only the jagged piece of mirror into which she gazes and sees herself young again. Skarmen's Risen have come to the House of Amorite to retrieve the fragment of mirror, which is its mistress's only joy.

This location is intended to be visited by the Acolytes whilst the Skarmen's Risen are in the process of retrieving the fragment of mirror. It is possibly the first time the Acolytes will have faced the Risen on their own and without extra aid, depending on how the attack on the Judiciary played out. Therefore, it is a potentially very dangerous fight for them. It also reveals or at least confirms to them the fact that they are trying to retrieve pieces of a broken mirror.

There are two possible ways in which the Acolytes might be drawn to the house of Amorite. The first is if they have realised that those responsible for the murders are seeking fragments of a broken mirror and learn that Lady Amorite owns such a fragment. This may be through contacts in the nobility or Eupheme Tassel. The second (and more likely) is when the attack is in progress being reported to the Acolytes by Constantine, and with the city is rising disorder and panic, there is no one else to come to Amorite's aid. Thanks to the Risen's slow battering down of the ancient Manse's defences, the Acolytes can make it to her Manse in time to intervene if they hurry.

LOCATION DETAILS

The House of Amorite sits on the edge of the cliff above the water of the Saint's Mouth in District VII (The Shadow Manses). Within a high stone wall lies a grand, three-story house built of pale stone and roofed in black slate amidst a tangle of undergrowth; its windows sealed by shutters, and its surface crawling with thick vines. The double iron gates have been forced open and the driveway is churned with heavy footprints. The slip gates and main doors to the manse have both been broken in by brute force and two ancient guardian servitors lay in pieces just beyond it; their tarnished brass components still twitching.

The interior of the house is dark, with only vague shapes of rooms and furniture visible (modifiers for Darkness apply as per page 198 of the **DARK HERESY** Rulebook). The use of lamp packs or other illumination reveals ghostly shapes of grand furniture, portraits, and artefacts all draped in thick cobwebs. The house smells of dust and neglect. The Acolytes hear screams and the sound of struggle from upstairs. Following the noise leads them to a great room that is poorly lit by a candelabra held in the hand of a terrified old woman

dressed in a tattered lace dress. Her hair is long, white, and wild. She is screaming in terror at a ring of cloaked figures that are slowly closing on her. Just behind her on a metal stand sits a piece of mirror like a jaded crescent moon, its surface reflecting the flickering light of the candles.

THE ATTACKERS

The attackers are the Risen (see pages 63-64 in Appendix I: NPCs and Antagonists) and there are a number equal to half the number of Acolytes plus one which has begun to mutate, though GMs should feel free to vary the number of attackers as needed. Skarmen's walking dead are wholly intent on getting the fragment of mirror and escaping with it rather than engaging the Acolytes—though they fight to the death to accomplish their goal.

LADY AMORITE AND HER SERVANTS

Lady Amorite is utterly terrified, but her already fragile mind refuses to let go of the one joy in her life—her mirror. She fights to the death for it, and more than likely, she is killed before the Acolytes can do anything about it unless they are particularly swift in coming to her defence. If necessary, use the Ruined Noble entry on page 66 in Appendix I: NPCs and Antagonists to represent Lady Amorite. Should she survive the attack, she falls into a catatonic state from which she does not recover.

Burning Down the House

As combat begins, Lady Amorite drops the candelabra, which ignites the cobweb-covered furnishings instantly. The fire begins as a blaze approximately a meter square. It then spreads at a rate of 1d5+1 meters a round and eventually engulfs the house, burning it to the ground. The exact rate that the fire spreads may be varied by the GM. All those within the fire or within close proximity (1m as a guideline) must follow the rules for being exposed to fire as per page 210 of the **Dark Heresy** Rulebook.

Who has the Mirror?

It is possible that either the Risen or Acolytes are in possession of the mirror at the end of the combat. If the Acolytes are in possession of it, they become a target for Skarmen's plans until they retrieve it, which modifies events accordingly, as they become the daemon's next target. In its desperation to recover the fragment, the daemon may force Skarmen's hand into moving precipitously and revealing the corrupted marshal's true colours.

If neither side manages to retrieve the fragment before the House of Amorite burns down, the fragment proves to have been completely unmarked and undamaged by the fire and may be retrieved from the cooling ashes—something that Skarmen's Risen try to do at the earliest opportunity.

Encounter Trigger Event: The Death of Xiabius?

Should the Acolytes require further spurring into action or if Skarmen has only one or two fragments of the mirror left to steal, there is one last trigger event that plunges Sinophia to the very precipice of cataclysm: the assassination of Xiabius Khan.

The Beginning of the End

Skarmen makes sure the Acolytes and the bulk of the Arbiters are distracted elsewhere before using sorcery to slaughter the Arbiters left in the Folly and animates their corpses to serve as his troops for a final battle. If the Acolytes possess some of the mirror fragments, this is his opportunity to try and draw them into his trap, where he can slay them and pick the shards from their corpses at his leisure.

Garbled reports start to come through on the vox of an attack on an Enforcer column moving through the Commercia ambushed by unknown forces. Rapidly, things worsen; some reports claim that Khan himself has been killed in the attack, others suggest that he is critically injured or even taken captive.

Tense minutes elapse, and slowly, certain facts begin to become clear: A Chimera carrying the Enforcer General to oversee the purging of District XIII by Sanctum Forces was struck and disabled by a missile, and the Enforcers guarding the column were gunned down in droves by heavy weapons fire.

The trickle of vox-traffic becomes a flood of contradictory reports on the Enforcer channels; some claim that the Undertow was responsible, whilst others say that the Adeptus Arbites themselves led the attack. Still others claim that the attackers are walking dead men. Shortly afterwards, loud explosions can be heard and plumes of smoke rise up from the Sinks and the Shadow Manses, whilst reports flood in of rioting, looting, and Enforcer teams going on berserk rampages among the people.

A great storm gathers over the city, and baleful green lightning flickers overhead. A final "recall to base" code flashes on the Acolytes' vox before all signals are drowned out by the what sounds like continuous, triumphant howling.

Note: The storm raging over Sinphia Magna is an unnatural tempest that blocks all astro-telepathic signals and interferes with long-range vox communication. Essentially, the city is now cut off completely from any help.

Part III: Through the Shattered Mirror

With anarchy blooming on the streets of Sinophia Magna, can the Acolytes stop Skarmen before he frees the Mirror Daemon?

State of Turmoil— Mayhem

The demise of Enforcer General Khan at the hands of Skarmen's unnatural minions has loosed the last restraints from the Enforcers and removed the last barrier of order. The population has already reached a boiling point of rumour-fueled fear and simmering violence. With the death or attempted assassination of Xiabius Khan, the Enforcers are shorn of all direction and become a headless beast lashing out and savaging the city at random. With no check on their panic, the population of Sinophia Magna begins to tear the city apart. Nobles barricade themselves within their mansions and open fire all that approach, or make for the starport in a desperate attempt to get off-world. Only a raging storm keeps the city from utterly destroying itself, and moving through the city's turbulent streets becomes a deadly trial.

With the Adeptus Arbites mysteriously inactive, all authority in the city is essentially paralysed by shock, furthering the quick spiral into annihilation.

GAME EFFECT

In essence, the city is in the midst of a full-blown civil breakdown. All attempted Inquiry Tests are Very Hard (–30) and all Intimidation attempts that are based on authority are Hard (–20).

Any attempt to move through the city takes far longer than it should, unless the Acolytes have managed to secure air transport or armoured vehicles. Also, crossing any major thoroughfare runs the risk of being caught up in running battles between the Enforcers and the Undertow. Looting, drunken revelries, or ongoing riots make the streets busy and dangerous. (See Rioters on page 66 of the NPCs and Antagonists Chapter).

SIGHTS AND SOUNDS

In the sky above the city, dark storm clouds boil, flashing with eerie green lightning, and a great wind drives the sound of screams and pleading through the streets with great sheets of rain. Thunder roars every few moments to shake the shutters of the buildings. Despite the storm, bands of rioters and madmen roam the streets, and the sound of gunfire (close and distant) is constant. Here and there bodies lie sprawled on street corners. Some streets are choked with crowds of desperate people trying to flee the city, and the electric smell of the storm fills the nose and mouth with the iron-tinged taste of blood.

ENDGAME

Unless the Acolytes have managed to solve the mystery and move against Skarmen earlier, things are now looking very bleak for Sinophia Magna. At this stage, the last pieces of the mirror are all either in Skarmen's hands or likely with the Acolytes, and he must either take them from them or conduct the joining ritual to free the Mirror Daemon. In either case, matters have become urgent, and the Acolytes must take the battle to their mysterious foe at last.

OPTIONAL ENCOUNTER: A FINAL BETRAYAL

If the Acolytes have reached this stage and still do not realise who is behind the murders, or alternately, if they are still in possession of a mirror fragment, then a final betrayal is dealt to them by Skarmen. They receive a signal to rendezvous with Adeptus Arbites forces at a road junction near the Celestine Wharf. If Constantine is not with them, he is also signaled to the location. They are met by a black Arbites Rhino APC which has clearly recently been in combat. Unless met by violence, the Rhino pulls up and four armoured and armed Arbitrators disembark, visors down and weapons at the ready. After spreading out and marking their targets, they open fire, looking to gun down Constantine first, then the Acolytes.

These are Skarmen's Arbites Corpse Minions (see page 64).

ENCOUNTER: THE BROKEN TOWER

As anarchy reigns in Sinophia Magna, the Acolytes' only chance is to stop Skarmen, which means getting into the tower of Haarlock's Folly to prevent him freeing the Mirror Daemon. There are then two main ways this can be done: by assault and by stealth. A further complication is that unless they have managed to glean the information, they do not know where in the tower the mirror is—although stiffening opposition the higher they go may well clue them to this. They may focus instead simply on killing Skarmen.

In terms of assistance, the Acolytes can rely on Constantine if he still lives and a handful of surviving uncorrupted Arbites he can round up to help them. Also depending on how they have conducted themselves previously in the adventure, it is time for the Acolytes to cash in a few favours: The Undertow, the Sanctum Enforcers, even perhaps private guards from a noble's cadre might perhaps be prevailed upon to lend assistance. In each case, this might only be a single squad of troops at best, given the anarchy and bloodshed in the city. However, each extra gun at the Acolytes' command might well make the difference.

THE OPPOSITION

Within the tower, Skarmen is engaged in completing the ritual re-construction of the mirror. If a full assault is underway, he pauses to direct the defences and unleash the Mirror Daemon (see page 58) to protect the upper levels. At this stage, the tower's defenders should be scaled somewhat by the GM as an appropriate challenge for the Acolytes and any aid they are able to bring to bear, compared with how well they have done in combating Skarmen's plan and servants prior to this also playing a part.

Note: If the Acolytes have not recovered any of the mirror fragments at the start of this final encounter with Skarmen, then he should be carrying the final shard on his person. He has recovered this last piece by sending his Risen to ambush the Enforcer General, Eupheme Tassel, or any other piece that the Acolytes missed.

At Skarmen's command are likely to be a number of Risen equal in numbers to the Acolytes (the GM should feel free to add or subtract to this number based on the Acolytes' condition, equipment, and rank), all of which are now mutated, as well as a dozen or more Arbites Corpse Minions and several gun servitors from his former command. In the depths below, Adept Talanis and his servitors remain ready to butcher any who intrude on his domain.

If necessary, Constantine can round up 2d5 Arbitrators to assist with the raid on Haarlock's Folly. These Arbitrators are the last few who were on patrol or otherwise away from the Folly, thus escaping Skarmen's dire influence. For their profile, use the Arbitrator on page 336 of the **DARK HERESY** Rulebook.

The GM should be aware that if the Mirror Daemon is unleashed upon the Acolytes that the battle can become extremely deadly. Holy or force weapons are the most effective against the Mirror Daemon, and it is likely that there are few such weapons amongst the Acolytes. One of the members of Spectre Cell 17 carries a force weapon, so if the GM wishes, he can have these NPCs appear during the final battle to assist the Acolytes.

By Assault

Taking the Folly by storm is going to be a dangerous and costly endeavour, even with outside assistance. The Arbites Corpse Minions and the remaining Risen are dug in behind fortified walls. It is up to the GM to run this battle as he sees fit, but as always he should place the focus on the Acolytes' actions towards its outcome.

By Stealth

A more profitable plan of attack is to use stealth, using the cover of the storm or a feigned attack by supporting forces to conceal the Acolytes' approach and to gain entrance through the ventilation shafts to the cellar levels. From there, the Acolytes can work their way up from the inside and either assault Skarmen directly or drop the defences to allow reinforcements to pour in before the final assault up the tower. In either case, Skarmen is a powerful opponent, particularly backed by the Mirror Daemon, and the Acolytes should be prepared for a serious fight in order to defeat him.

OPTIONAL ENCOUNTER: INTERVIEW WITH THE DAEMON

Even with Skarmen dead and his servants destroyed, there remains the small matter of the daemon and the mirrors. In the secret chamber at the top of the tower, the Acolytes find them both, one whole and the other missing only one more piece to complete it (the number of missing pieces should change depending on how many shards the Acolytes may have recovered).

The spectral image of the daemon awaits within its glass prison, a half-seen liminous face with a mocking and almost sardonic expression. It's power (for the moment) is expended, and the daemon is (relatively) helpless.

If they listen, the daemon talks to them, offering them a very simple and very reasonable deal: Free it from its prison, and it will depart in peace to the warp, but not before soothing the raging chaos its black arts have enraged in Sinophia Magna and returning the city to relative peace. It will also answer their questions if it can, although the shackles Haarlock placed on it prevent it from uttering too many truths. If the Acolytes take the bargain, they each gain 1d5+5 Corruption Points.

If they do not listen, all they need to is to break the mirror again, and it collapses into the thirteen fragments once more, sending the daemon back into the dark glass to await its master in silent dread. Each Acolyte gains a permanent Fate Point and a powerful, immortal enemy.

The Daemon's Answers

Should the Acolytes agree to its bargain, it might provide them with the following information and, if released, follows through on its commitment to pacify Sinophia Magna.

The daemon freely answers any question pertaining to its binding, its plot with Skarmen, and the murder victims.

The daemon admits that it desires to be free so it might flee before Haarlock, "returns to plunge these stars of Calyx in to an abyss that none, not even my kind, can escape."

If asked what Haarlock wanted or where he went after shattering the mirror, the Daemon shudders in pain and answers through clenched jaws, "Beyond the void of night, to change what was and master what can be, and from thence he now comes, returning from where no man nor god returns unchanged. Seek the Blind Tesseract if you would chart his course…" However, it can offer nothing else, its image visibly weakened by the effort of talking.

Arriving Early

It's possible that the Acolytes have worked out that the Adeptus Arbites are suspect and that Skarmen is behind it all long before he can attack Xiabius or even perhaps kill the Judiciary, although this is unlikely. This early resolution will be rewarded by the fact that Skarmen will not have had time to slaughter the remaining Arbiters at the Folly and re-animate their bodies, greatly reducing the number of Risen he can mobilize against the Acolytes—although more Risen are hiding in the catacombs to call on if he has not yet expended them. Matters may also be clouded by the fact that without irrefutable evidence of corruption, many of the surviving Arbites will remain loyal, and a number are already too far gone to turn, meaning that it will still be a deadly battle to stop Skarmen.

RESOLUTION

If the Acolytes are successful (whether nor not the daemon is freed or the mirror is shattered), the storm breaks and washes away the blood from the streets for now. Constantine (if he lives) takes over what remains of the Adeptus Arbites force, calling in his scant reinforcements from Karib City and sending a distress call to his subsector command. After learning of the daemon's plot and Skarmen's infamy—even if the common people never do—the Undertow and the Enforcers alike rein in their forces for the time being.

It is made known some days later that Xiabius Khan yet lives, although he is now a wrecked man, broken in body and spirit. The Acolytes will see him again before they depart Sinophia on an Inquisitorial transport, as they receive ceremonial golden maces in gratitude for their services to Sinophia before a closed session of the newly restored Quorum. The awards are presented with some delight by the smiling new Judiciary, the honoured Cal Sur'Maywroth. In addition, each Acolyte is granted 1,000 throne gelt and is given the Sinophian Bloodlaurel, a special commendation medal that is the highest that Sinophia has to offer.

REWARDS

Experience awards are given after each of the three parts of **DAMNED CITIES** or at other convenient lulls during play. Each Acolyte should receive between 100 and 300 xp per game session, with bonuses awarded for particularly good bits of deduction and for fully engaging with the adventure's plot.

III

APPENDIX

NPCs and Antagonists

•

Maps of Haarlock's Folly

•

Player Handout

•

The Haarlock's Legacy Campaign

Appendix I: NPCs and Antagonists

Major NPCs

This appendix is divided into two parts. The Major NPCs section details and describes the other characters who play an important role in the plot of **Damned Cities**. As such, they are each detailed individually. The people and creatures listed in the Masses section reflect instead general types of NPCs that may be encountered in Sinophia Magna.

Note: For all the following NPC's, all melee attacks are considered to have the character's Strength Bonus added in.

Arbitrator Precinct Marshal Colchis Skarmen

Precinct Marshal Skarmen is an imposing and distinguished figure whose grey hair and beard does not hide the fit, muscled form beneath his black carapace armour. His manner is firm and commanding. He will try to present himself as a no-nonsense, tough, reasonable, and pious veteran of service to the Golden Throne, but as matters progress this mask will begin to slip, revealing hatred, prejudice, and malevolent wrath lurking beneath the surface. Behind Skarmen's eyes also lurks the power and implacable will of his daemonic master, whose dark arts combined with Skarmen's own martial skills make him a formidable opponent indeed.

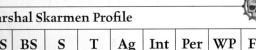

Marshal Skarmen Profile

WS	BS	S	T	Ag	Int	Per	WP	Fel
43	48	48	48	35	40	50	70	36

Movement: 3/6/9/18 **Wounds:** 22
Skills: Athletics (S), Awareness (Per) +10, Command (Fel) +10, Common Lore (Adeptus Arbites) (Int) +10, Common Lore (Underworld) (Int) +10, Deceive (Fel) +20, Dodge (Ag) +10, Forbidden Lore (Daemonology, Heresy, Warp) (Int) +20, Interrogation (WP) +10, Inquiry (Fel), Intimidate (S) +10, Invocation (Wp) +10, Literacy (Int), Psyniscience (Per) +20, Scholastic Lore (Judgement) (Int) +10, Scrutiny (Per) +10, Speak Language (Low Gothic) (Int), Speak Language (High Gothic) (Int).
Talents: Basic Weapon Training (Bolt, SP), Disarm, Melee Weapon Training (Primitive, Shock), Psy Rating 4, Pistol Training (Bolt, SP, Las), Takedown.
Sorcery: Boil Blood (21), Compel (19), Distort Vision (10), Fearful Aura (9), Sense Presence (9), See Me Not (16), Suggestion (11).
Mask of Seeming: See page 243 of the **Dark Heresy** rulebook.
Armour: Carapace (Arms 6, Body 6, Legs 6).
Weapons: Bolt pistol (30m; S/2/—; 1d10+5 X; Pen 4; Clip 8; Reload Full, Tearing), shock maul (1d10+34 I; Shocking).
Gear: Micro-bead, photo visor, respirator, 2 bolt pistol clips, frag grenade, Arbites ward accessor, encrypted data-slate.

SORCERY!

Though not a true psyker, Colchis Skarmen has been corrupted and touched by a powerful daemon of the warp, who has gifted the fallen Marshal with sorcerous power. Each of Skarmen's psychic powers (regardless of the actual focus time) take at least a full round to employ and have a threshold +2 higher than they would have had for a psyker. Also, the practice of the dark arts is far from safe, even compared to the use of a psyker's abilities, and he must add +5 to the results of any Psychic Phenomena and Perils of the Warp he incurs.

The Daemon in the Mirror

If the Mirror Daemon's plan reaches near-fulfilment and only one or two of the fragments of the mirror remain to assemble the shattered glass, it will grow strong enough to manifest a spectral presence outside its prison. Even though this is a merest sliver of the daemon's power, it can still make for a terrifying opponent if its wrath is provoked.

Thanks, however, to Haarlock's bindings, it cannot leave the Folly, nor can it or anyone it possesses touch the fragments of the mirror.

If the daemon is reduced to zero Wounds, it is not destroyed. Instead, it flees howling in outrage back to the mirror and cannot manifest itself again for 1d5 hours.

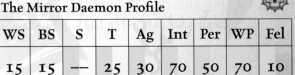

The Mirror Daemon Profile

WS	BS	S	T	Ag	Int	Per	WP	Fel
15	15	—	25	30	70	50	70	10

Movement: 3/6/9/18 **Wounds:** 8
Skills: Awareness (Per) +10, Deceive (Fel) +20, Forbidden Lore (Daemonology, Heresy, Warp) (Int) +20, Psyniscience (WP) +20, Speak Language (all) (Int) +20.
Talents: None.
Traits: Daemonic (TB 4), Fear (Frightening) 1, Flyer 6, From Beyond, Incorporeal*, Possession, Psy-Rating 5, Spirit Form, Warp Instability.
Powers (Psy Rating 5): Boil Blood (21), Compel (19), Distort Vision (10), Fearful Aura (9), Sense Presence (9), See Me Not (16), Suggestion (11)
Note: The Daemon Shade does not suffer perils of the Warp.

IMPROVED NATURAL WEAPONS (TRAIT)

This creature's attacks are powerful enough to crush plasteel or punch through armour. The creature's natural weapons no longer count as Primitive.

* Incorporeal: Strong energy fields and consecrated barriers block the daemon and it is vulnerable to psychically charged or holy attacks and powers.

Spirit Form: The fragment of the daemon is visible to normal sight only as an insubstantial and balefully luminous shadow, making any attempts to attack it, shoot it, or divine its presence suffer a basic −10 penalty. It can be seen normally via Psyniscience or other Psychic Powers (such as Sense Presence) and detected by devices that can register warp disturbance.

ARBITRATOR ADJUTANT FIHAD CONSTANTINE

Fihad Constantine is a young Arbitrator whose primary role is to act as adjutant to Precinct Marshal Skarmen. Inexperienced but possessing a keen intelligence, he is a very recent arrival on Sinophia and was unsettled enough by recent events to get a report off-world, even though it was not approved by the Precinct Marshal. Able and spirited, Constantine is a devoted servant of the Imperium who may rise high in the service of the Emperor if he survives long enough…

Fihad Constantine Profile

WS	BS	S	T	Ag	Int	Per	WP	Fel
33	38	38	38	41	40	38	38	37

Movement: 3/6/9/18   **Wounds:** 14
Skills: Athletics (S) +10, Awareness (Per), Charm (Fel), Dodge (Ag), Drive (Ground Vehicle) (Ag), Common Lore (Adeptus Arbites) (Int) +10 Common Lore (Underworld) (Int), Interrogation (WP) +10, Literacy (Int) +10, Scholastic Lore (Judgement) (Int) +10, Scrutiny (Per), Speak Language (Low Gothic, High Gothic) (Int) +10, Swim (S).
Talents: Basic Weapon Training (Bolt, SP), Disarm, Melee Weapon Training (Shock), Pistol Training (Bolt, SP), Takedown.
Armour: Carapace (Head 6, Arms 6, Body 6, Legs 6).
Weapons: Bolt pistol (30m; S/2/—; 1d10+5 X; Pen 4; Clip 8; Reload Full, Tearing), hand cannon (35m; S/—/—; 1d10+4 I; Pen 2; Clip 5; Reload 2 Full), mono-knife (3m; 1d5+3 R; Pen 2).
Gear: Micro-bead, photo visor, respirator, 1 bolt pistol re-load and 1 hand cannon re-load, Arbites ward accessor.

ENFORCER GENERAL XIABIUS KHAN

Xiabius Khan is a former bounty hunter and the current head of the Enforcers of Sinophia Magna. A slab-muscled brute with a taste of crass opulence, he is cunning, vicious, and very dangerous. Khan's position is bound to the noble houses of Sinophia, who pay him and give him legal authority. He is most satisfied with the license for his violent pleasures and the wealth that his position has brought him, and he will fight to the death to keep it.

Enforcer General Khan Profile

WS	BS	S	T	Ag	Int	Per	WP	Fel
43	45	40	35	45	38	41	35	25

Movement: 4/8/12/24   **Wounds:** 17
Skills: Awareness (Per) +10, Common Lore (Imperium) (Int), Concealment (Ag), Dodge (Ag), Drive (Ground Vehicle) (Ag), Inquiry (Fel), Interrogation (WP) +10, Intimidate (S) +20, Medicae (Int), Security (Ag), Shadowing (Ag), Silent Move (Ag), Speak Language (Low Gothic) (Int), Tracking (Int).
Talents: Basic Weapon Training (Bolt, Las, SP), Disarm, Hip Shooting, Melee Weapon Training (Chain, Primitive, Shock), Nerves of Steel, Pistol Training (Bolt, Las, SP), Rapid Reaction.
Armour: Enforcer light carapace (Head 5, Arms 5, Body 5, Legs 5).
Weapons: Bolt pistol (30m; S/2/—; 1d10+4 X; Pen 4; Clip 12; Reload Full), chainsword (1d10+5 R; Pen 2; Balanced, Tearing), hand cannon (35m; S/—/—; 1d10+4 I; Pen 2; Clip 5; Reload 2 Full), shock maul (1d10+3 I; Shocking).
Gear: Dress uniform overcoat, medals and gorget of office, 3 bolt pistol clips, 3 hand cannon clips, photo-visor, respirator, manacles, override ward accessor.

HESUL, TIBER, AND SCORN: THE RAG-KINGS OF SINOPHIA MAGNA

The so-called 'Kings in Rags' are Sinophia's brutal criminal underworld masters. One does not run into one of the Kings unless they wish it—and if you do, no doubt they mean to turn you to their favour, or lead you to an early grave. Each has a kingdom of drinking dens, lost warehouses of smuggled goods, brothels, and streets which owe them protection. All constantly move from place to place in their kingdoms accompanied by their most trusted muscle and clad in muddy and tattered remnants. The three most powerful Rag-Kings are Hesul, Tibre, and Scorn, who together make up the ruling Rag Court which holds sway over the lesser kings and their criminal vassals.

HESUL

Hesul is a tall woman with long lank hair woven through with tattered ribbons of dark green. Utterly ruthless, she is very perceptive but prefers to reserve judgement on matters that are not clear.

Hesul Profile

WS	BS	S	T	Ag	Int	Per	WP	Fel
23	28	30	30	40	37	47	55	30

Movement: 4/8/12/24   **Wounds:** 19

Skills: Awareness (Per), Carouse (T), Climb (S), Common Lore (Underworld) (Int) +20, Common Lore (Imperium) (Int), Command (Fel) +10, Concealment (Ag) +10, Deceive (Fel) +10, Dodge (Ag) +10, Evaluate (Int), Inquiry (Fel), Intimidate (S) +20, Security (Ag), Secret Tongue (Undertow) (Int) +20, Shadowing (Ag), Silent Move (Ag) +10, Speak Language (Low Gothic) (Int).

Talents: Basic Weapon Training (SP), Melee Weapon Training (Basic, Primitive), Pistol Training (Las, SP), Rapid Reaction, Sprint.

Armour: Flak jacket (Arms 3, Body 3).

Weapons: Four mono-knives (3m; 1d5+3 R; Pen 2), compact stub automatic (15m; S/3/—; 1d10+2 I; Pen 0; Clip 4; Reload Full) with silencer, 2 spare clips, 2 frag grenades.

Gear: Red rag cloak, iron jewelry.

TIBER

Tiber is a hugely muscled killer with a fearful temper and a loose mouth from which oaths and crude jokes flow with equal ease. He is disposed to action, usually violent, and dislikes those who are not simple in what they say. If he thinks someone is playing him as a fool, they will die painfully.

Tiber Profile

WS	BS	S	T	Ag	Int	Per	WP	Fel
38	22	45	40	30	23	30	25	20

Movement: 3/6/9/18   **Wounds:** 15

Skills: Awareness (Per), Carouse (T), Common Lore (Underworld) (Int) +20, Common Lore (Imperium) (Int), Command (Fel) +10, Deceive (Fel), Intimidate (S) +20, Secret Tongue (Undertow) (Int) +20, Speak Language (Low Gothic) (Int), Trade (Tanner) (S).

Armour: Patched carapace (Arms 4, Body 5, Legs 4).

Talents: Iron Jaw, Melee Weapon Training (Chain, Primitive).

Weapons: Brass knuckles (1d5+3 I; Primitive, Unbalanced), chainaxe (1d10+8 R; Pen 2; Tearing), hand cannon (35m; S/—/—; 1d10+4 I; Pen 2; Clip 5; Reload Full).

Gear: Flayed skin cloak.

SCORN

Scorn is a bitter old man whose watery eyes and stained beard bely a cruel and keen intelligence. Scorn chain smokes lho sticks, coughing and wheezing all the while, and speaks little unless to make a sour remark or ask a penetrating question.

Scorn Profile

WS	BS	S	T	Ag	Int	Per	WP	Fel
25	25	21	23	30	47	30	35	30

Movement: 3/6/9/18   **Wounds:** 10

Skills: Awareness (Per), Barter (Fel) +10, Chem-Use (Int) +10, Command (Fel) +10, Common Lore (Underworld) (Int) +20, Common Lore (Imperium) (Int), Deceive (Fel) +10, Evaluate (Int) +10), Literacy (Int), Logic (Int), Scrutiny (Per) +10, Secret Tongue (Undertow) (Int) +20, Speak Language (High Gothic, Low Gothic) (Int), Trade (Apothecary) (Int).

Talents: Melee Weapon Training (Primitive), Pistol Training (Las, SP).

Armour: Mesh vest (Body 3).

Weapons: Compact laspistol (15, S/—/—; 1d10+1 E; Shots 15; Reload Full; Reliable), psi-jammer (see Inquisitors Handbook), blade concealed in walking cane (10+2 R, Pen 2).

Gear: Black rag cloak, walking cane that conceals a hidden mono blade, lho sticks.

THE HONOURED MARGRAVE CAL SUR'MAYWROTH

Cal Sur'Maywroth is a lean man with an unwholesome, hungry glitter in his dark eyes. Just as his painted face and perfumed skin hide the rot beneath, so too are his precisely measured manners those of someone utterly confident not only of his superiority but of the inferiority of all others. Beneath the layers of lace and brocaded fabric, the Margrave's flesh is wasted away, and he lives by virtue of the augmetics bestowed on him by his wealth and position. Although the duelling days of his youth are long over, ever watchful for threats to his life, Cal Sur'Maywroth carries a power blade concealed in his ornate obsidian walking cane and a needler tucked in a hidden, velvet-lined pocket.

Cal Sur'Maywroth Profile

WS	BS	S	T	Ag	Int	Per	WP	Fel
37	31	23	21	22	44	51	45	37

Movement: 2/4/6/12   **Wounds:** 8

Skills: Awareness (Per) +10, Blather (Fel), Carouse (T), Charm (Fel) +20, Command (Fel) +10, Common Lore (Imperium) (Int) +10, Deceive (Fel) +20, Evaluate (Int) +20, Forbidden Lore (Heresy) (Int), Gamble (Int) +10, Literacy (Int) +10, Scrutiny (Per) +10, Speak Language (High Gothic, Low Gothic) (Int) +10.

Talents: Autosanguine, Exotic Weapon Training (Needle Pistol), Melee Weapon Training (Power, Primitive), Pistol Training (Las, SP).

Armour: Mesh woven coat (Arms 3, Body 3, Legs 3).

Weapons: Compact needle pistol (15m; S/–/–; 1d10-1 R; Pen 0; Clip 3; Reload Full, Accurate, Toxic), serpentine power blade (1d0+4 E; Pen 6; Fast, Power Field).

Gear: Fine clothes and jewelry, basic bionic locomotion, good bionic respiratory system, ward accessor ring (Quorum Member, Clockwork Court), personal encrypted vox.

THE SAGACITY EUPHEME TASSEL

Eupheme Tassel is the pale and sullen Keeper of the Roles, Sinophia Magna's official records of government. Despite the elaborate grey robes and dark veil of her office which makes her appear far older than her years, Eupheme is a young woman of noble birth and poetic temperament. Worn to distraction by the drudgery of her calling, her sunken eyes mask a quick and incisive mind. In the dark watches of the night, however, Eupheme Tassel pours over incomplete copies of proscribed works, and her dreams are helped along by night dust in search of a release from the rigidity of her duty-bound life.

Eupheme Tassel Profile								
WS	BS	S	T	Ag	Int	Per	WP	Fel
16	18	24	37	34	51	38	37	31

Movement: 3/6/9/18   **Wounds:** 12

Skills: Awareness (Per), Common Lore (Imperium, Administratum) (Int) +20, Common Lore (Ecclesiarchy, Imperial Creed) (Int) +10, Common Lore (Adeptus Arbites, Underworld) (Int), Ciphers (Occult) (Int), Forbidden Lore (Heresy) (Int), Literacy (Int) +20, Scholastic Lore (Bureaucracy, Judgement) (Int) +10, Scholastic Lore (Archaic, Philosophy, Occult) (Int), Speak Language (High Gothic, Low Gothic) (Int) +20, Trade (Copyist) (Int) +10.

Talents: None.

Armour: Vestments of office (Body 2, Arms 1, Legs 1).

Weapons: Razor letter opener (1d5).

Gear: Ornate grey robes, black veil, writing kit of superior quality, parchment, data-slate, official seal, ward accessor ring (lesser, Clockwork Court), 2 pinches of night dust.

LYNAN YANTRA

Lynan is a hab-worker and drifter whose few decades of life have been spent trying to make a living by heating scrap for the traces of precious substances within. His years of toil and the toxic fumes of the scrap furnaces have left him weak and in poor health, so that he appears prematurely old and withered.

Lynan Yantra Profile								
WS	BS	S	T	Ag	Int	Per	WP	Fel
15	18	23	18	21	27	35	21	25

Movement: 2/4/6/12   **Wounds:** 7

Skills: Awareness (Per), Common Lore (Imperium, Underworld) (Int), Speak Language (Low Gothic) (Int), Trade (Scap-Gleaner) (Int).

Talents: None.

Armour: None.

Weapons: None.

Gear: Drab citizen's garb, faded green Sinophian cloak stained with chemical burns, 2 Thrones.

SPECTRE CELL 17

Spectre Cell 17 is a Tenebrae Collegium kill-team that has been sent to eliminate the Acolytes and erase any dangerous material relating to the Erasmus Haarlock's relationship to the Tyrant Star. Spectre Cell 17 consists of four highly trained Inquisitorial operatives who will track down the Acolytes and ambush them, confirm the identity of their kills, and depart.

HELLOS

Hellos is a former Arbitrator and the principal agent within Spectre Cell 17. Grim, highly intelligent, and focused on the mission's success, he is a remorseless and untiring hunter.

Hellos Profile								
WS	BS	S	T	Ag	Int	Per	WP	Fel
40	44	38	43	35	40	34	43	30

Movement: 3/6/9/18   **Wounds:** 16

Skills: Athletics (S), Awareness (Per) +10, Ciphers (Tenebrae Collegium) (Int) +10, Deceive (Fel) +20, Dodge (Ag) +10, Common Lore (Underworld) (Int) +10, Forbidden Lore (the Inquisition) (Int) +10, Interrogation (WP) +10, Inquiry (Fel) +20, Literacy (Int), Scholastic Lore (Judgement) (Int) +10, Scrutiny (Per) +20, Secret Tongue (Tenebrae Collegium) (Int) +20, Speak Language (High Gothic) (Int), Speak Language (Low Gothic) (Int).

Talents: Ambidextrous, Basic Weapon Training (Bolt, SP), Disarm, Labyrinth Conditioning, Melee Weapon Training

(Primitive, Power, Shock), Pistol Training (Bolt, SP), Quick Draw, Takedown, Two-Weapon Wielder (Ballistic and Melee).

Armour: Enforcer light carapace (Arms 5, Body 5, Legs 5).

Weapons: Bolt pistol (30m; S/2/—; 1d10+5 X; Pen 4; Clip 8; Reload Full, Tearing), power sword (1d10+8 E, Pen 6, Balanced, Power Field).

Gear: Storm coat, photo-contacts, respirator, micro-bead, stunner, 2 reloads for bolt pistol.

JONAS DRAY

Prior to being recruited into the service of the Inquisition, Jonas Dray was a trooper in the elite divisions of the hardened Gunmetallican regiment of the Imperial Guard. Born in the Infernis, Dray has fought since he could lift a weapon. His natural endurance combined with the training lavished on him by the Tenebrae Collegium has made him a soldier of terrifying ability.

Jonas Dray Profile

WS	BS	S	T	Ag	Int	Per	WP	Fel
38	48	47	50	36	20	35	35	20

Movement: 3/6/9/18   **Wounds:** 18

Skills: Awareness (Per), Carouse (T), Ciphers (Tenebrae Collegium) (Int), Common Lore (Imperium) (Int), Common Lore (War) (Int) +10, Deceive (Fel) +10, Dodge (Ag), Drive (Ground Vehicles) (Ag) +10, Forbidden Lore (the Inquisition) (Int), Intimidate (S) +10, Literacy (Int), Secret Tongue (Tenebrae Collegium) (Int) +10, Speak Language (Low Gothic) (Int).

Talents: Basic Weapon Training (SP, Las, Bolt), Iron Jaw, Jaded, Labyrinth Conditioning, Melee Weapon Training (Chain, Primitive), Nerves of Steel, Pistol Training (Las, SP), Rapid Reload, Resistance (Fear, Psychic Powers), True Grit, Unshakable Faith.

Armour: Storm trooper carapace (Head 6, Arms 6, Body 6, Legs 6).

Weapons: Boltgun (90m; S/2/—; 1d10+5 X; Pen 4; Clip 24; Reload Full, Tearing) fitted with red-dot laser sight, hand cannon (35m; S/—/—; 1d10+4 I; Pen 2; Clip 5; Reload 2 Full), chainsword (1d10+6 R; Pen 2; Balanced, Tearing), 2 frag grenades (12m; S/—/—; AP 0; 2d10 X; Pen 0; Clip 1; Blast (4)), 2 blind grenades (12m; S/—/—; AP 0; —; Clip 1; Smoke).

Gear: Storm coat, infra-red goggles, photo-contacts, respirator, micro-bead, stunner, 2 reloads for boltgun.

ARKADIA FLAVION

Arkadia Flavion is an assassin who learnt her deadly art from the Sons of Dispater before being recruited into the service of the Tenebrae Collegium. Athletic and highly skilled, Arkadia Flavion can disappear into the tangle of rooftops and blow the back of a target's skull out without him even realising she is there.

Arkadia Flavion Profile

WS	BS	S	T	Ag	Int	Per	WP	Fel
33	51	35	31	44	37	38	31	32

Movement: 4/8/12/24   **Wounds:** 12

Skills: Athletics (S) +10, Awareness (Per) +10, Climb (S) +20, Concealment (Ag) +20, Ciphers (Tenebrae Collegium) (Int) +10, Deceive (Fel) +20, Dodge (Ag) +20, Common Lore (Underworld) (Int), Forbidden Lore (the Inquisition) (Int) +10, Intimidate (S), Literacy (Int), Secret Tongue (Tenebrae Collegium) (Int) +10, Security (Ag) +20, Silent Move (Ag) +20, Speak Language (High Gothic) (Int), Speak Language (Low Gothic) (Int).

Talents: Basic Weapon Training (SP, Las, Bolt), Crack Shot, Labyrinth, Conditioning, Melee Weapon Training (Primitive), Peer (Nobility), Peer (Underworld) Pistol Training (Bolt, SP, Las), Sharpshooter.

Armour: Synskin (Head 2, Arms 2, Body 2, Legs 2).

Weapons: Angelus bolt carbine (100m; S/—/—; 2d10 X; Pen 5; Clip 3; Reload 3 Full, Accurate, Tearing) fitted with a telescopic sight, hand cannon (35m; S/—/—; 1d10+4 I; Pen 2; Clip 5; Reload 2 Full).

Gear: Cameleoline cloak, storm coat, synskin, photo-contacts, respirator, micro-bead, stunner, 6 extra rounds for bolt carbine.

LO-TAN

Lo-tan is a product of the Templar Calix of the Scholastia Psykana and is a warrior psyker of terrible ability and ruthless efficiency. Clad in a high-collared storm coat, his face covered with a blank mask of tarnished silver, he is an instrument of death wielded at the command of the Tenebrae Collegium.

Lo-tan Profile

WS	BS	S	T	Ag	Int	Per	WP	Fel
41	23	38	34	51	30	27	48	23

Movement: 5/10/15/30   **Wounds:** 14

Skills: Acrobatics (Ag) +20, Awareness (Per), Ciphers (Tenebrae Collegium) (Int) +10, Deceive (Fel) +10, Dodge (Ag) +20, Forbidden Lore (the Inquisition) (Int) +10, Forbidden Lore (Psykers) (Int) +10, Literacy (Int), Secret Tongue (Temple Calix) (Int), Secret Tongue (Tenebrae Collegium) (Int) +20.

Talents: Assassin's Strike, Blademaster, Blind Fighting, Combat Master, Labyrinth Conditioning, Melee Weapon Training (Primitive, Power), Pistol Training (Las, SP), Psy-Rating 3, Resistance (Fear, Psychic Powers), Sure Strike, Strong Minded, Swift Attack.

Psychic Powers: Distort Vision, Fire Bolt, Float, Flash Bang, Sense Presence, Spasm, Wall Walk, Weapon Jinx.

Armour: Hardened body glove and mesh cowl (Head 3, Arms 3, Body 3, Legs 3).

Weapons: Force sword (1d10+6** R, Pen 5**, Balanced), power blade (1d10+6 E, Pen 6, Power Field).

Gear: Storm coat, photo-contacts, respirator, micro-bead, stunner.

** *Includes Strength bonus and bonus for psy-rating*

FORCE WEAPONS

Made from the rarest materials and interlaced with psy-reactive and channelling circuitry, force weapons are capable of channelling the mental power and aggression of a psyker. Unless wielded by a psyker, force weapons simply count as a Good Craftsmanship Mono variant of their standard primitive weapon type. However, in the hands of a wielder with a Psy Rating, the weapons are much more. For every point of Psy Rating the wielder has, the force weapon's Damage and Penetration increases by +1 (these bonuses are already added into Lo-tan's stats).

In addition to normal damage, whenver a psyker damages an opponent with a force weapon, he may, as a Free Action, channel psychic will into the blade. Treat this effect as a power with Threshold 6. On a success, the wielder and the victim make Opposed Willpower Tests; if the attacker wins, the victim suffers an additional 1d10 points of Energy Damage ignoring armour and Toughness Bonus, plus an additional 1d10 for each degree of success.

LABYRINTH CONDITIONING

The mind of an agent trained by the Tenebrae Collegium is a carefully constructed maze of shutouts and thought dams designed to thwart the attempts of others who would learn the agent's secrets. The psyker character gains a +10 bonus on Deceive Tests when being questioned and to resist anyone using the Intimidate Skill on him. He also has a +10 bonus to Willpower to resist Interrogation and mind reading effects such as Mind Scan. In the case of a Psychic Power or effect, this bonus can be combined with bonuses to resist Psychic Powers from other Talents.

THE MASSES

This section details rules for the unnamed masses that form a crucial part of **DAMNED CITIES**. Many of the entries are root entries that can be modified, turning them into various different adversary subtypes all based on the same root. The GM can simply apply the bonuses, penalties and skill changes to the root entry to create a new adversary subtype. Also, note that many of the NPCs listed in the **DARK HERESY** rulebook are perfectly usable and useful in this setting, most particularly the Citizen, Dissolute Noble, Dreg, Heavy, Lurker, and Scum.

Critical Damage and the Masses: When running a combat involving NPCs and antagonists from the following section, it is recommended that the GM apply rules for Sudden Death Critical Hits (see page 201 of **Chapter VII: Playing the Game** in **DARK HERESY** for details).

THE RISEN DEAD

These animate cadavers used by Skarmen are the corpses of murder victims who were held in the precinct mortuary in the cellars of Haarlock's Folly. Animated and controlled by sorcery, these unhallowed things are walking corpses, filled with malignant energy, their dead flesh and rotting eyes hidden by the ubiquitous hooded cloaks of Sinophia Magna. Skarmen has been using these minions to recover the pieces of mirror and eliminate any obstacles to his plan to free the daemon. Unlike some foul creatures the Acolytes may have encountered in the past, these creations are extremely potent, extraordinarily strong, and resilient to injury thanks to the powers bound within them. They are also intelligent and possessed of daemonic cunning.

Risen Profile

WS	BS	S	T	Ag	Int	Per	WP	Fel
40	20	(10) 55	(8) 40	20	30	15	45	10

Movement: 2/4/6/8   **Wounds:** 25

Skills: Awareness (Per).

Talents: Resistance (Psychic Powers), Melee Weapon Training (Primitive).

Traits: From Beyond, Fear 1 (Disturbing)**, Dark Sight, Natural Weapons (Dead Hands), Psychic Static*, Unhallowed, Unnatural Strength (x2), Unnatural Toughness (×2) and Walking Dead.

Armour: Sigil-stitched flesh (2 Body, Arms, Legs, Head), plus any worn.

Weapons: Dead hands (1d10+10 I, Primitive), may instead use weapons as needed.

Gear: Hooded cloaks and rags that smell of rot and caustic chemicals.

Walking Dead: These creatures do not need to breathe. They do not tire and are immune to poisons and diseases, as well as many environmental hazards. They do not suffer the effects of being Stunned nor the penalties for being injured. In addition, only Damage suffered to the Head or Body is counted—any suffered to an Arm or Leg is simply disregarded, other than Critical Damage, which will just render the limb useless.

TABLE: 3-1: RISEN MUTATIONS

Roll	Result
01–20	**Twisted:** The Risen's appearance is mutated to better reflect the daemon within, granting it the Frightening Trait.
21–40	**Hungry:** The Risen's teeth and nails have extended to become razor-sharp fangs and claws, gaining it the Improved Natural Weapons Trait.
41–60	**Poison Bile:** The Risen's skin and saliva weeps caustic poison, causing its natural attacks to become Toxic.
61–80	**Brute:** The Risen's flesh pulses with contorted power, increase Strength and Toughness by +10.
81–90	**Death Scream:** Instead of attacking normally, the Risen may unleash a terrifying howl echoing in the warp. All characters without the From Beyond Trait within 50m must immediately pass a **Difficult (–10) Willpower Test** or become Stunned for 1d5 Rounds.
91–00	**Dark Fire:** The Risen's empty eye sockets and mouth burn with coruscating dark energies. The character counts as being equipped with a hand flamer with unlimited ammunition.

Unhallowed: Blessed and Holy weapons inflict double Damage after the effects of armour are taken into account.

*Psychic Static: The daemon's influence creates a perpetual field of psychic white noise around the character. This functions in exactly the same way as the White Noise minor Psychic Power (see page 168 of the **DARK HERESY** rulebook) but is always in place and requires no Psychic Test. The power always has a range of 50m. It can also be ended and started again without a psychic test.

**The Risen's Fear Trait only comes into play if it is obvious that the Risen are the walking dead. This Trait has no effect if the Risen are disguised, hidden, or otherwise do not appear out of the ordinary.

Mutated: The chaotic energy bound within the dead flesh of these creatures begins to manifest itself as twisted alternations to their cadaverous bodies over time. If one of the Risen is listed as being Mutated, roll on Table 3–1 and apply the effects listed to its profile.

ARBITES CORPSE MINIONS

Should the daemon's final plan come to fruition, it will command Skarmen to kill the few Adeptus Arbites remaining under his command and bind their corpses as unhallowed minions. Although lesser in power compared to the carefully bound Risen, these grey-fleshed and milky-eyed soldiers will be sent to kill Xiabius Khan, retrieve the final fragment of mirror, eliminate the Acolytes, and defend the tower during the daemon's resurrection.

Arbites Corpse Minion Profile

WS	BS	S	T	Ag	Int	Per	WP	Fel
30	30	40	40	30	20	25	30	18

Movement: 3/6/9/18   **Wounds:** 15

Skills: Awareness (Per).

Talents: Resistance (Psychic Powers), Melee Weapon Training (Primitive, Shocking), Pistol Training (Las, SP), Basic Weapon Training (Las, SP).

Traits: From Beyond, Dark Sight, Natural Weapons (Dead Hands inflicting 1d5+SB I, Primitive), Unhallowed and Walking Dead (see Risen profile).

Armour: Storm trooper carapace (Head 6, Arms 6, Body 6, Legs 6).

Weapons: Combat shotgun (30m; S/3/—; 1d10+4 I; Pen 0; Clip 18; Reload Full; Scatter), hand cannon (35m; S/—/—; 1d10+4 I; Pen 2; Clip 5; Reload 2 Full), shock maul (1d10+5 I; Shocking).

SINOPHIAN KILLER

Killers come in many forms throughout the events of **DAMNED CITIES**, but all are dangerous individuals inclined and equipped to do the Acolytes violent harm.

Sinophian Killer Profile								
WS	BS	S	T	Ag	Int	Per	WP	Fel
35	35	35	35	30	28	30	30	28

Movement: 3/6/9/18
Wounds: 12

Skills: Awareness (Per), Carouse (T), Common Lore (Imperium) (Int), Common Lore (Sinophia) (Int), Deceive (Fel), Intimidate (S), Speak Language (Low Gothic) (Int).
Talents: Melee Weapon Training (Primitive), Pistol Training (Las, SP), Basic Weapon Training (Las, SP).

Enforcer of the Judiciary's Court

The Enforcers sworn to the Judiciary's court have become the agents of the nobility's need to hold onto prestige and power as the world withers around them. Most are greedy or vicious men and women whose sins have been given official sanction. Clad in vulcanized storm coats, the enforcers are well equipped and brutal in approach.

Characteristics: As Killer, except +5 to Ballistic Skill, Weapon Skill, and Intelligence.
Skills: As Killer, plus Athletics (S), Common Knowledge (Sinophia) (Int) +10, Interrogation (WP).
Talents: As Killer.
Weapons: Punisher chastisement baton (1d10+3 I), Stub auto loaded with dum-dums (30m; S/3/—; 1d10+5 I; Pen 0; Clip 9; Reload Full). If the State of Turmoil has increased to Boiling Point (see page 49), Enforcers will also carry a lasgun with an overcharge pack (100m; S/3/—; 1d10+4 E; Pen 0; Clip 30; Reload Full), 1 frag and 1 photon flash grenade. Large squads will also have one trooper in ten armed with grenade launchers or webbers.
Armour: Light flak coat (Arms 2, Body 2, Legs 2).
Gear: Two reloads for each weapon carried, vox, photo-visor.
The Mandato: Members of this feared organisation add an additional +5 to Willpower, gain the Jaded Talent, and are equipped with two doses of stimm and an injector.

Mouthpiece

Family members of Sinophia's nobility rarely deal directly with outsiders except under circumstances of carefully choreographed formality. Contact and control of a family's affairs are left to the mouthpieces—trusted servants bound to the family by blood oaths and trained at great expense from an early age. Culled from servants, business negotiators, estate managers, and (if necessary) bodyguards, the smooth-mannered mouthpieces are as close as most get to the merchant nobles.
Characteristics: As Killer, except +10 Agility, +10 Intelligence, and +10 Fellowship.
Skills: As Killer, plus Barter (Fel) +10, Charm (Fel) +10, Command (Fel), Deceive (Fel) +20, Evaluate (Int) +10, Logic (Int), Literacy (Int), Security (Ag), Speak Language (High Gothic) (Int), and Scrutiny (Per) +10.
Talents: As Killer, plus Quick Draw.
Weapons: Compact laspistol (15m, S/—/—; 1d10+1 E; Shots 15; Reload Full; Reliable), monosword (1d10+3 R; Pen 2, Balanced).
Armour: Hardened body glove (Arms 3, Body 3, Legs 3).
Gear: Fine clothes, personal encrypted vox, seal of merchant noble family, data-slate, and one hotshot pack for laspistol.

Undertow Muscle

The Undertow is omnipresent in Sinophia Magna's lower districts. The so-called Rag-Kings enjoy employing ex-PDF thugs who have fallen on hard times after discharge. Such men are usually tough and willing to do the Rag-King's dirty work for their next hit of obscura or simply to avoid the hopelessness of their lives. Cloaked and hooded in tattered green, they blend into the rain-soaked streets and watch quietly from broken windows and shadowed doorways. Though often poorly equipped, they are hardened killers and stubborn fighters.
Characteristics: As Killer.

Skills: As Killer, plus Athletics (S), and Deceive (Fel) +10.
Talents: As Killer, plus Basic Weapons Training (Flamer).
Weapons: Knife (3m, 1d5+2 R; Primitive) and either barbed iron cudgel (1d10+4 I; Primitive) or stub revolver (30m; S/—/—; 1d10+3 I; Pen 0; Clip 6; Reload 2 Full; Reliable) or pump shotgun (30m; S/—/—; 1d10+4 I; Pen 0; Clip 8; Reload 2 Full; Scatter) or improvised flamer (10m; S/—/—; 1d10+3 E; Pen 2; Clip 4; Reload 2 Full; Flame, Unreliable).
Armour: Rag-tag body armour (Body 2, Legs 2, Primitive).
Gear: Green cloak with gang patches, 1d5 thrones.

DENIZEN OF SINOPHIA MAGNA

Sinophia Magna's population is as numerous and diverse as any other long-settled Imperial World, although most outsiders would consider them unusually wary, duplicitous, and impious by culture.

Denizen of Sinophia Magna Profile								
WS	BS	S	T	Ag	Int	Per	WP	Fel
20	20	30	30	30	35	30	30	30

Movement: 3/6/9/18   **Wounds:** 10
Skills: Carouse (T), Common Lore (Imperium) (Int), Deceive (Fel), Speak Language (Low Gothic) (Int).
Talents: None.

Drunk

In Sinophia Magna there is little hope, and many find what they can at the bottom of a bottle. Befuddled and confused drunks are well disposed (perhaps a little too much so) towards those who buy them more drink and are always willing to talk and share rumours.
Characteristics: –10 WS, Ag, and WP.
Skills: As Denizen, plus Carouse (T) +20.
Talents: None.
Weapons: None.
Armour: None.
Gear: Half empty bottle of 'gyn, ragged and stinking cloths.

Rioter

Rioters are ordinary citizens of Sinophia Magna who have been driven by fear and anger to rise up in violent protest. Though poorly armed, rioters are still dangerous when driven into a frenzied rage.
Characteristics: As Denizen.
Skills: As Denizen.
Talents: Frenzy, Melee Weapon Training (Primitive).
Weapons: Improvised weaponry (1d10+1 I, Primitive, Unbalanced), 25% chance of 1 fire bomb (9m; S/—/—; AP 0; 1d10+3 E; Pen 6; Clip 1; Blast (3)), or nail bomb (9m; S/—/—; AP 0; 1d10+1 X; Pen 0; Clip 1; Blast (2), Unreliable).
Armour: None.
Gear: Various ragged clothes and assorted tatters.

Ruined Noble

The nobility of Sinophia is ridden with lost fortunes and pawned inheritances. Many scions of what were great and worthy families are now reduced to little more than beggars clothed in the tattered finery of their more fortunate forefathers.
Characteristics: –15 WP.
Skills: As Denizen, plus Blather (Fel), Charm (Fel), Deceive (Fel) +10, Gamble (Int), Literacy (Int), Sleight of Hand (Ag), Speak Language (High Gothic) (Int).
Talents: Jaded.
Weapons: None.
Armour: None.
Gear: Worn and stained finery.

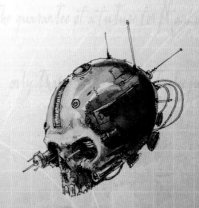

CLASSIFICATION: DARK OMEGA
DATE: 5301815.M41
SUBJECT: Recent Occurrences in Sinophia Magna

My Loyal Acolytes,

Contained herein this astropathic message is a report received by the court of the Arbitrator Lord Marshal via astropathic transmission from the world of Sinophia.

The report is from Fihad Constantine, adjutant to the Arbitrator Precinct Marshal of Sinophia. The report attached outlines a series of violent attacks on members of the Sinophian nobility.

As you may well know, under usual circumstances, the murder of a prominent citizen would not be worthy of a priority astropathic transmission—nor of the Holy Ordos' concern or of your involvement. However, the nature of the attackers might indicate a malefic aspect to the crimes, and Sinophia's past means all is suspect. Furthermore, there are other reports from this long-troubled world indicate that it tips ever closer the abyss of misrule and calamity, and these murders could provide a cataclysm for civil disorder and rebellion between the city's ruling factions.

Mark the details of the attached report and take every inference to heart. You have my authority to lay open this matter, investigate whether these are simple murders or the shadow of a greater heresy in the making, and take actions such as are necessary for its removal. I am also granting you use of the rosette if it is deemed necessary you must reveal your actions to the populace at large; the Arbites are aware of your impending arrival and your association with me.

+++

Arbites Summation Reports

Source: Sinophia Magna, Sinophia
Subject: Murder of Viscount Hiram Sur'Seculo
Summary of occurrence:

Viscount Hiram Sur'Seculo was the head of House Seculo, a worthy and renowned house of Sinophia. The Viscount and his party had returned home to his manse in District VII just after nightfall, when it appears they were attacked without warning. From the destruction at the scene, it is clear that the attackers ripped through the doorway with force and it is possible they may have sustained some damage in doing so, though no blood from the attackers could be found at the scene.

There were no surviving witnesses, though it can be deduced that there were at least four to eight attackers in the murders. Psychic auto-séances confirm this.

The Viscount, his bodyguard, and five servants were killed by being beaten and/or torn apart, evidencing a level of physical force greater than that of normal human limits. The attackers also looted the personal rooms of the Viscount. The destruction was considerable, and it was unclear what the attackers were seeking, nor whether they succeeded in finding what they sought. Many valuables were left scattered in disarray in the premises, some of considerably high value.

Various security devices and recording equipment at the Viscount's manse inexplicably failed during the attack, only to resume working the attack had passed. Tech-adept examination can offer no explanation for this.

Cross reference addendum to report:

There have been at least two further attacks on members of the Sinophian noble and mercantile class. In both cases, the victims were beaten and rent apart, and in at least one other, there has been an attendant robbery.

We are asking for the Holy Ordos' investigations in this matter, and I am sending this report per regulation regarding such matters. Upon arrival on Sinophia, agents of the Conclave need only seek me out at our newly-acquired precinct hall at the tower known locally as Haarlock's Folly. I await your guidance in this matter.

I remain a loyal servant of the Imperium and the God-Emperor,

Arbitrator Adjutant Fihad Constantine

++++

HAARLOCK'S FOLLY

EXTERIOR

SECRET CHAMBER

SKARMEN'S OFFICE

ELEVATOR to 1ST FLOOR

ELEVATOR to CELLAR

GROUND FLOOR

ELEVATOR to 2ND FLOOR

1ST FLOOR

2ND FLOOR

HAARLOCK'S
FOLLY
– CELLARS –

ELEVATOR TO
GROUND FLOOR

MORGUE CHAMBER
#I

UNUSED
CHAMBER

CONVERTED
MORGUE

CONCEALED DOOR

THE HAARLOCK LEGACY CAMPAIGN

DAMNED CITIES is part of an arc of adventures which together forms the Haarlock Legacy campaign arc: an open, modular campaign whose parts, save for its conclusion, can be played (with some modification) in any order. The campaign's individual adventures surround dark events and domains of a long-vanished and infamous Rogue Trader, Erasmus Haarlock, and the dreadful power various factions hope to gain from his Legacy. Other adventures in the Haarlock Legacy Campaign are The House of Dust and Ash (found in DISCIPLES OF THE DARK GODS), TATTERED FATES, and DEAD STARS.

By playing the adventures in the campaign, the Acolytes are drawn into a spiraling whirlpool of catastrophe and begin to piece together the true horror of what is about to be unleashed on the Calixis Sector. Whilst other adventures within the campaign yield information about Erasmus Haarlock's motivations and tragic past, DAMNED CITIES gives Acolytes pursuing the mystery of the Legacy the secret of what it was that he was seeking before he vanished.

A LEGACY OF TERROR

The Rogue Trader House of Haarlock is an ancient one, far predating the Calixis Sector that it helped to found. For thousands of years, the Haarlock warrant gave the dynasty license to travel far beyond the Imperium and to bring death and war to anything they deemed a threat to mankind's place in the cosmos. Over their centuries of conquest, they put whole

DARK PATTERNS

In the Haarlock Legacy campaign, certain stylistic themes have been employed that link it and the other parts of the campaign together. GMs, when adding their own encounters and adventures to the campaign, are encouraged to include their own take on these themes and symbols:

- Countdowns, clockwork, and the manipulation of time
- The number 13
- Bereavement and loss
- Bloodlines and the sins of the past haunting the present
- The mastery of flesh and matter—ancient dark science
- Bitter vengeance and insane obsession
- That which was long buried, forgotten, or hidden now awakening
- Servants fearing their master's return
- The dark traveller

THE BLIND TESSERACT AND THE CLIMAX OF THE CAMPAIGN

Erasmus Haarlock's beloved family was slaughtered by his own kin in a vicious war for the inheritance of the Haarlock Rogue Trader warrant. This event drove Erasmus to hunt down and kill all others of his line and to seek a means of undoing the past so that those who had been taken from him could be returned. The means of achieving this insane and impossible desire drove Erasmus Haarlock in his inscrutable plans. He discovered that there was a place that he could go to learn the means to achieve his desire. This place could only be reached by plotting a course into a far and terrible place, a course that could only be plotted from the Blind Tesseract, a secret place hidden deep within the forbidden planet Mara. This fact is the revelation that will draw Acolytes to Mara and the climax of the campaign.

The GM can introduce this revelation into DAMNED CITIES if he intends to run DEAD STARS as the campaign finale in the near future. If, however, DAMNED CITIES is the first adventure the group has played as part of the campaign, or if the GM wishes to play other adventures before the Acolytes reach the climax, then he can keep this revelation back and introduce Mara as the confirmed location of the Blind Tesseract into a later part of the ongoing campaign.

worlds to the sword and plundered the tombs of xenos races passed to dust before man first walked upon the Earth. They acquired terrible secrets and amassed dark lore, weapons, and trinkets enough to found a dozen empires of their own and condemn them in the eyes of the Imperium a thousand times over. The protection of the warrant and the secrecy with which they guarded their affairs within the Imperium kept them safe for millenia. The Haarlock line was ever a fractious one, and betrayal and internecine warfare were as common among the Haarlocks as were the twin sparks of diabolic genius and insanity that warred in the natures of the greatest of them. It was in such a family conflict that one of the lesser sons of the line was to come to the fore, his destiny burning like a bloody star in the heavens.

Erasmus Haarlock slaughtered his blood kin, unified the powers and dark lore that his line had amassed over the millennia, and willed them to a single purpose, a terrifying project that spanned a dozen worlds and brought into play arts and sciences forbidden since elder days. Then, at the height of his labours with all in preparation but for the final piece of the puzzle, Erasmus Haarlock vanished.

Now, hundreds of years since that day, the stars have again turned, and on a dozen worlds the ancient domains of the House of Haarlock flicker to life. Strange events and mysterious deaths occur, and things long-buried awake. Signs and portents plague the visions of seers and the tortured dreams of madmen across the Calixis Sector, and their import disturbs the councils of the powerful and the power-hungry alike. Visions of worlds set to burn in cold fire, of a device that can order the very fabric of reality to its master's will, of a howling voice in the void and a black sun rising. Dreams of the traveller's return…

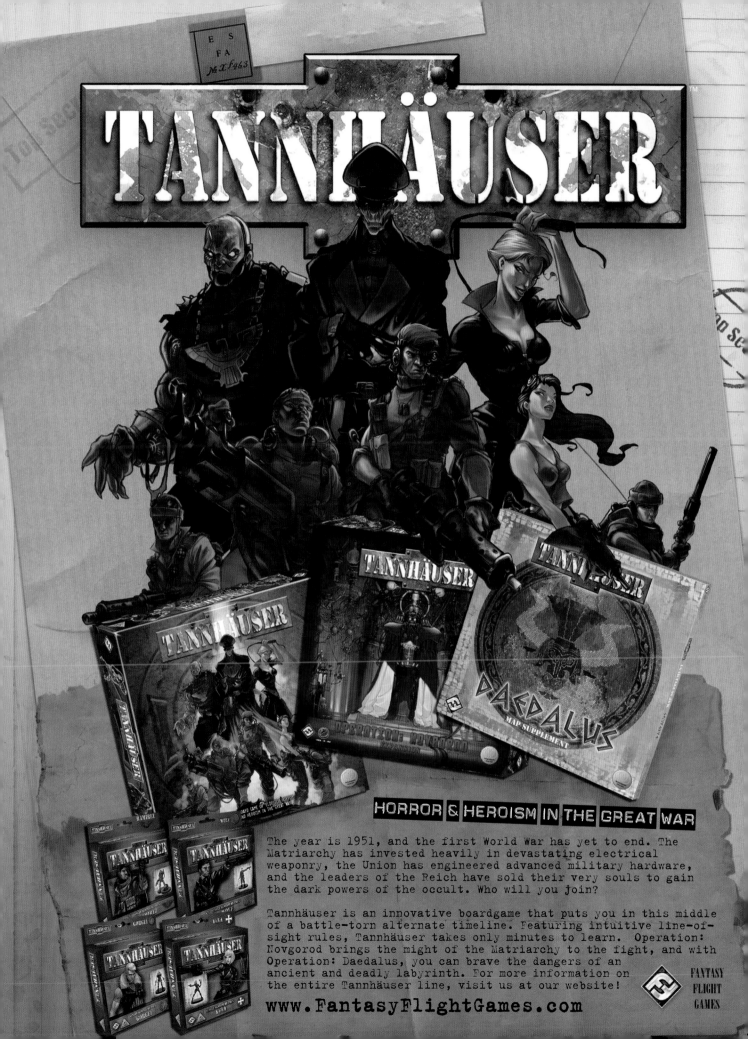